The Complete Handbook for Ministers

The Complete Handbook for Ministers

James L. Christensen

Fleming H. Revell Company
Old Tappan, New Jersey

Library of Congress Cataloging in Publication Data

Christensen, James L.
    The complete handbook for ministers.

    1. Pastoral theology—Handbooks, manuals, etc.
I. Title.
BV4016.C48   1985   264   84-22916
ISBN 0-8007-1403-2

TO
those close colleagues in the ministry:
Carlton, Sheldon, Jim, Monroe, Dan,
Allan, Charles, and Clyde

CONTENTS

PREFACE

For years I have been sharing materials with other pastors for their worship and pastoral responsibilities. By and large, the materials have been used by me in my own congregations, but they also have been in demand by many denominational and independent clergymen and lay ministers. For a while, the innovative contemporary approach was popular; now there is a return to the traditional. Persistent requests still are made for several of the books which are out of print.

This volume has taken choice and frequently requested usable materials from several of my books now out of print and from some in print. New material has been added where it seemed appropriate. It blends both the traditional and contemporary approaches. Obviously the limitation of space has made brevity imperative. May this concise handbook become a constant companion to many servants of Christ.

JAMES L. CHRISTENSEN

Section 1

WORSHIP

WORSHIP WORTHY OF GOD

"O magnify the Lord with me, and let us exalt his name to-gether" (Psalms 34:3). This is the purpose of public worship.

There is only one audience—it is God. The worship is not religious entertainment for the gathered congregation. It is not focused primarily on the people. Worship is God-centered. It is a recognition of God's presence and love, and a human expression of appreciation. Worship is declaring God's greatness and worth.

Therefore, to worship meaningfully is a supreme achievement. It is a spiritual experience. The act of public worship is an attempt to give worthy expression to a personal, loving God whose highest revelation was in Jesus Christ. It includes an awareness of fellowship with Him with adoration and praise. It includes a receiving and a clarification of His will. It involves a response of offering and giving of self to a more devoted commitment. Such expressions are made as corporate acts.

This section of the book is designed to help the leaders of public worship, primarily in nonliturgical churches. Both traditional and contemporary types of material are included to meet the varied tastes and practices among the churches. No demand for uniformity is expected, so that denominational and nondenominational ministers may benefit.

CALLS TO WORSHIP

1

Whosoever thou art that enterest this church, be silent, be thoughtful, be reverent, for this is none other than the House of God.

2

To worship is to quicken the conscience by the holiness of God, to feed the mind with the truth of God, to purge the imagination by the beauty of God, to open the heart to the love of God, to devote the will to the purpose of God.

3

You who through worship would find God, know ye not that God this very hour is seeking you? Lay before Him now a mind open to all truth, a spirit attuned to the whisper of the still small voice, a heart responsive to the cries of human needs, and a will committed to the walking of His way: then you shall go forth a soul renewed, exalted, ennobled, empowered, for our Great God is a Giver Supreme.

4

To all who mourn and need comfort, to all who are weary and need rest, to all who are friendless and wish friendship, to all who pray and to all who do not but should, to all who sin and need a Saviour, and to whomsoever will, this church opens wide the door and in the name of Jesus bids you welcome.

5

Be still, and know that I am God. I am exalted among the nations, I am exalted in the earth (Psalms 46:10).

6

My soul longs, yea, faints for the courts of the Lord; my heart and flesh sing for joy to the living God (Psalms 84:2).

7

Wait for the Lord; be strong, and let your heart take courage; yea, wait for the Lord (Psalms 27:14).

8

O come, let us worship and bow down, let us kneel before the Lord, our Maker. For he is our God, and we are the people of his pasture, and the sheep of his hand (Psalms 95:6–7).

9

Extol the Lord our God, and worship at his holy mountain; for the Lord our God is holy (Psalms 99:9).

10

Serve the Lord with gladness! Come into his presence with singing! Enter his gates with thanksgiving, and his courts with praise! Give thanks to him, bless his name! For the Lord is good; his steadfast love endures for ever, and his faithfulness to all generations (Psalms 100:2, 4, 5).

11

This is the day which the Lord has made; let us rejoice and be glad in it (Psalms 118:24).

12

I lift up mine eyes to the hills. From whence does my help come? My help comes from the Lord, who made heaven and earth (Psalms 121:1–2).

13

I was glad when they said to me, "Let us go to the house of the Lord!" (Psalms 122:1).

14

Our help is in the name of the Lord, who made heaven and earth. . . . The Lord is near to all who call upon him, to all who call upon him in truth (Psalms 124:8; 145:18).

15

Seek the Lord while he may be found, call upon him while he is near; let the wicked forsake his way, and the unrighteous man his thoughts; let him return to the Lord, that he may have mercy on him; and to our God, for he will abundantly pardon (Isaiah 55:6–7).

16

The Lord is in his holy temple; let all the earth keep silence before him (Habakkuk 2:20).

17

Your Father knows what you need before you ask him. . . . But seek first his kingdom and his righteousness, and all these things shall be yours as well (Matthew 6:8, 33).

18

Draw near to God and he will draw near to you (James 4:8).

19

Ask, and it will be given you; seek and you will find; knock, and it will be opened to you (Matthew 7:7).

20

Come to me, all who labor and are heavy-laden, and I will give you rest. Take my yoke upon you, and learn from me; for I am gentle and lowly in heart, and you will find rest for your souls (Matthew 11:28–29).

21

The hour is coming, and now is, when the true worshipers will worship the Father in spirit and truth, for such the Father seeks to worship him. God is spirit, and those who worship him must worship him in spirit and truth (John 4:23, 24).

22

LEADER   We come to worship, not because it is a duty,
RESPONSE   But because it is a delight;

LEADER   Not because a minister calls us,
RESPONSE   But because God has called to us;
LEADER   Not to display to the world our fine garb,
RESPONSE   But to witness to the world our faith in God;
LEADER   Not to smirk at others because of our goodness,
RESPONSE   But to search together for God's righteousness;
LEADER   Not to be complimented for our proficiency,
RESPONSE   But to hear the Word speak to our deficiency;
LEADER   Not to listen as others are condemned,
RESPONSE   But to be told how we have sinned;
LEADER   Not to be satisfied with knowing religious rules,
RESPONSE   But to surrender all to the Kingom's rule;
LEADER   Not to take away whatever God will give us,
RESPONSE   But to go away fitted for service;
UNISON   We would encounter the God who searches for us.

23

THIS IS THE DAY

This is the day the Lord has made,
Like yesterday, and the day before!
This is a day for loving and dreaming,
A day for knowing that
"God's in His heaven," for heaven is on earth, too,
Right here—right now.
This is a day for forgiving
And being forgiven,
And for beginning again—
A day for singing and praying,
Resolving, renewing, rejoicing!
With so much to celebrate,
And so much to share,
Let us praise God together,
As we find ways to serve Him
And our fellowman.

SAMUEL F. PUGH[1]

24

LEADER We have come here
in the name of the Father who made us,
in the name of the Son who makes us free,
in the name of the Spirit who makes us one.

PEOPLE Let us worship God, the Father; God, the Son; and God the Holy Spirit.

25

LEADER Worship is a congregation joyfully singing, praying, giving, celebrating God's gift of Jesus Christ to all mankind.

PEOPLE Worship is a group of young adults sharing their convictions concerning the deepest meanings of the Christian life.

LEADER Worship is a gathering of young people using new songs, new rhythms, new ways to express their own ideas.

PEOPLE Worship is the dedication of a moment or a lifetime to an awareness of the presence of God.

LEADER Worship is the never-ending search for the will of God and the joy of feeling that a person or a group has found it, even for one fleeting moment.

UNISON Worship is a corporate expression of gratitude, a unison prayer of penitence, a harmonious outburst of song in any spot where people have assembled in the spirit of Christ.

26

This is the day that the Lord has made!
This is a day in beauty arrayed!
This is a day with glory displayed!
This is a day!

This is a day worth its weight in gold!
This is a day with its wealth untold!
This is a day so good to behold!
Live while you may!

SAMUEL F. PUGH

INVOCATIONS

1

Almighty God, unto whom all hearts are open, all desires known, and from whom no secrets are hid; Cleanse the thoughts of our hearts by the inspiration of thy Holy Spirit, that we may perfectly love thee, and worthily magnify thy holy Name; through Christ our Lord. *Amen.*[2]

2

O Thou in whom we live and move and have our being; we offer and present to Thee our souls and our bodies, our thoughts and our desires, our words and our deeds, to be a living and continual sacrifice; through Jesus Christ our Lord. *Amen.*

3

Author of the world's joy, bearer of the earth's pain, friend of the thankful, counselor of the weak, hope of the aged, inspirer of the young: We dedicate to Thee our worship, and pray that Thou wilt replenish the reservoirs of our souls with Thy power and love. *Amen.*

4

Eternal God, who are beyond all our thoughts about Thee, higher than all the words we speak concerning Thee, and greater than all we confine in our emotions about Thee: We stand at attention to acknowledge Thee, and bow in humility to thank Thee, in the name of Jesus Christ by whom we know Thee. *Amen.*

5

Like ships storm-driven into port, like wanderers begging refuge from the darkness of night, like starving souls seeking living bread, like flowers turning to the sun, like prodigals seeking the father when all is spent: So we come to Thee seeking hope after fear, calm after storm, and rest after work. Satisfy our deeper longings with Thy presence and peace. *Amen.*

6

O Thou from whom, in whom, and for whom we are: We thank Thee that Thou hast made the world and us so that we cannot escape Thee and that Thou comest to us through every channel of expression, even though at times our reception is blurred with interference. Penetrate our delusions, shine through our spiritial deafness, interpret to us Thyself so that we may know Thee. *Amen.*

7

God our Father, the citadel of our thoughts, the foundation of our character, and the spring from which comes the water of life: We come to acknowledge Thee, to think Thy thoughts after Thee, to expose our souls to Thee, and to seek refreshment of spirit from Thee. *Amen.*

8

Almighty God, Thou has promised power to those whose lives are attuned to Thee: From the noisy, demanding ways of the business world to the calm of this sanctuary, dedicated to the life of the soul, we have come to gaze upon Thee and to recharge our sagging spirits. *Amen.*

9

O Thou who art found by those who truly seek Thee, known by those who love, and seen by those whose hearts are pure: Let us feel Thy presence in this sacred place. We bring to Thee the thirst we cannot quench at any earthly spring, and the hunger which alone is satisfied by Thy Word. Withdrawn in this place from the turmoil of the world, send us a blessing from above that will lift us out of fear into faith, and out of foolish ways into Thy ways. *Amen.*

10

We are thankful for Jesus, who has shown us that behind the veil of our vision beats a heart of love. So we have come here with our troubles and sorrows that we might find light for our darkness, assurance for our doubts, and peace for our nerves. In Jesus' name. *Amen.*

11

God, You are greater than all our names given You; larger than all our human symbols describing You; closer than the person sitting next to us; and more real than we realize. So we come to express to You our adoration in as many ways as we can. Through Jesus our Lord. *Amen.*

12

We come to You our God and our Father because You are the same from generation to generation. Yet when we listen to You there is always something new, something surprising, something startling in what You are saying to us. At times we are shaken. At times we are hurt. Yet we know we must still listen. And listening we learn that Your Word is always a living Word and that the work to which You call us is always a contemporary task. Give us ears to hear, and committed wills to know You. *Amen.*

13

Lord, help us to worship You with everything we've got in every part of our living. In our fellowship in the church as well as our witness in the world, save us from all that is second-rate and half-hearted. Praise be to you. *Amen.*

14

We are full of knowledge, but of You, Lord, we know all too little. We are always talking, but of You, Lord, we speak all too seldom. Teach us the beginning of wisdom and open our lips to speak Your praise. *Amen.*

15

Thank You, Lord, for strength to match our weakness, comfort to lighten our distress, guidance to lead us in perplexity, inner peace to hold us against disaster, love to dissolve our bitterness, and forgiveness to cover our failures. So much has been given to us. Help us to bring hope to the despair of others.

16

To men searching the night skies—You gave a star.
To shepherds on the whispering hills—You gave a voice.
To fishermen working on the shore—You gave greater work to
   be done.
What is Your sign for me, Lord?
Let me not be blind or deaf or resistant when You come.

PASTORAL PRAYERS

1

O God, the shepherd of Thy people through their earthly wanderings, who dost neither slumber nor sleep: We bow before Thee as sheep of Thy pasture. Beside the still waters, we now wait with Thee. We know not what the future has of "marvel or surprise," of green pastures or of valleys of dark shadows; whatever it be, be Thou our strength and shield.

We thank Thee for the shared joys, successes, and friendships that have blessed our church family. We remember in gratitude the bright hours of faith, the many examples of sacrifice, the depth of love demonstrated, the spiritual recoveries made, and the high moments when Thy Holy Spirit glowed within. Bless this congregation with harmony, rekindle its vision, and commit it anew to Thy mission.

Good Shepherd, fold us safely in Thy love, lest we be overtaken by storm, or lost in darkness, or, in carelessness or curiosity, wander from Thy care. Save us from following the clamor of the world. May we not forget that poverty and riches are of the spirit.

When age and infirmity overtake us, may we be found thankful for life and time's golden memories that are sweet and good. At eventide, when life's lamp is burning low, may we lie down safely in Thine eternal fold, to the glory of Jesus Christ in whom there is no separation. *Amen.*

2

O God of us all, whose wisdom is beyond the reaches of our minds, whose mercy is wider than our wanderings, and whose redeeming love is deeper than our sins: We bow in humility before Thee. By Thy goodness our souls are fed. By Thy truth our minds are enlightened. By Thy Son, Jesus Christ, we have forgiveness and life abundant.

O Lord, we confess that too much we have lived as if there were no God. We have followed our own way as if Jesus had never lived. We have dressed ourselves up outwardly without adorning ourselves inwardly. We have built fine mansions in which to live, but have not bothered to learn how to live. We have pursued the things that perish in the grasping, and have been indifferent to those treasures of the spirit in which there is eternal security. We have been serious over the trivial and trivial over the serious. O God, have mercy upon us, and forgive us.

O Lord God, may some insight pierce through our rationalizations to revive our hunger for Thee. Cause the music of the Gospel to stir the lost chords of our souls that a new song may be sung in our hearts. May Thy Holy Spirit burn through the sham of our excuses, melting away false barriers, rekindling love that has grown cold, and allowing the best in each one to have its way. May Jesus Christ and His Church have a more compelling claim upon our lives than ever before. Since we know not what a day may bring forth, and that the hour for obeying and serving Thee is present, give us the courage to yield to Jesus Christ today. *Amen.*

3

Lord, we are here today—in this place—not to try to escape from this community's problems, though we would like to! O God, how we would like to! We would like to withdraw into an

ivory tower, a safe distance away, behind high walls; then close
our eyes and our ears and our minds, and forget the turmoil
and war, strikes, and worldwide revolutions. We would like to
not be reminded of poverty and squalor, pain and death, and
pretend they do not exist. If we could just go about our
own pursuits uninterrupted and unconcerned. But God,
we can't!

Even now, we know the unreasonable demands, threats, and
the violence are but the cries of frustrated, unhappy, impatient
people—and we must listen. O Lord, You know the ill-
flavored words that have been hurled, the bitterness and jealousy that has poisoned life. Tempers are jagged and explosive.
Lord, many cities are like kegs of dynamite with the fuses ig-
nited. There could be a terrible outbreak of bloodshed even
right here. Lord, we've come to this church to get our calm, to
gain perspective, to pray for honesty enough to see and admit
injustice; to plead for wisdom to know what should be done;
and courage to urge it to be done. Above all, Lord, we're Your
"new humanity" that You have created to be peacemakers and
reconcilers. Then, guide our thoughts by Your thoughts and
our spirits by Jesus' Spirit, so that our actions might be Your
actions, in the name of peace. *Amen.*

4

O God, You know the desperate and relentless struggles of
persons known or unknown to us who need immediate help.
Believing that You are able to do much more than we can ask
or think, and that You respond to the wavelengths of our concerns and intercession, we place upon the altar for Your blessings these persons (*a period of silence after each request*).

Pray for:

A bereft soul for whom the heavens seem shut.

A daughter who has sacrificed her future and chances of marriage for the care of a widowed mother.

A used-car salesman torn between the ethical requirements of the Gospel and the demands of his employer to meet ruthless competition.

Anxious parents who have not heard from an absent child for two months or more—a daughter gone to work in a distant city; a son drafted into military service and now overseas; the youngest of their family away in college.

A clerk whose financial needs tempt him to filch from the cash register.

A stenographer whose job depends on humoring the whims of an amorous boss.

A man under cancer's death sentence.

A mother trying to rear her children respectably, when they all know that their father has no regard for either decency or law.

A family trying to live down a scandal that drove the oldest daughter to suicide.

An investor whose profitable ventures have inflated his pride and made him careless with others' trust.

A physician under pressure to write narcotics prescriptions for a patron to whom he is financially obligated.

A trusted employee who for months has been embezzling from his firm.

A high school youth torn between the license brashly advocated by his school's fraternity and the standards for which he has stood as officer in his church youth group.

A deacon enamored of the new office girl and beginning to play the fool.

A merchant seeing his little business, the work of half a lifetime, now declining under terrific competition from chain stores, which he cannot possibly meet.

A social aspirant in whose heart envy and ambition have joined forces and are running wild.

An elder for whom religion has gradually lost its vitality and significance and has degenerated into mere formality.

A teacher who has devoted a quarter of a century in dedicated service to the community becoming disillusioned because public education is made a political pawn.

O God, bring Your healing and salvation to these we implore, through Jesus Christ. *Amen.*

G. EDWIN OSBORNE[3]

5

Lord, let us do our work each day, and if the darkened hours of despair overcome us, may we not forget the strength that accompanied us in the desolation of other times. May we still remember the bright hours that found us walking over the silent hills of childhood or dreaming on the margin of the quiet river when the light glowed within us, and we promised our early God to have courage amid the tempests of the changing years. Spare us from bitterness and the sharp passions of unguarded moments. May we not forget that poverty and riches are of the same spirit. Though the world knows us not, may our thoughts and actions be such as shall keep us friendly with ourselves.

Lift our eyes from the earth and let us not forget the uses of the stars. Forbid that we should judge others lest we condemn ourselves. Let us not follow the clamor of the world but walk calmly in Your path. Give us a few friends who would love us for what we are.

And though age and infirmity overtake us and we come not within the sight of the castle of our dreams, teach us still to be thankful for life and time's golden memories that are good and sweet; and may the evening twilight find us gentle still, and keep ever burning before our vagrant steps the kindly light of hope. *Amen.*

SPECIAL PRAYERS

For Worship Leaders

FOR THE MINISTER

1

O God, my Heavenly Father, who hast called me to present Thy saving Gospel to men: Bless my preparation made for this hour. Forgive my failings, my lack of perception, my inconsistencies, my inadequacies, my neglect. Fill me now with Thy Holy Spirit. As I surrender myself to Thee, take Thou my voice and speak Thy pleading; take Thou my soul and make it a channel of Thy healing grace; take Thou my body and use it as an instrument of Thy will, to the honor of Jesus Christ, whose I am and whom I serve. *Amen.*

2

O Thou who hast placed Thy precious treasure in earthen vessels: Humble my spirit before Thee now with a vision of the magnitude of my task which is too great for me, and with a sense of unworthiness to represent Thee, and an utter dependence upon Thy grace and Holy Spirit. May all that I say and do now be done for Thy glory, not mine. May Thy love be communicated in words that will bring light to the confused, healing to the sorrowful, a quickened conscience to the comfortable, salvation to the lost, and the challenge of Jesus Christ to all. *Amen.*

For Others Who Assist

ORGANIST AND CHOIR

1

O God of beauty and harmony, in whose presence the heavenly choirs chant their chorales, and harps and trumpets resound as the voice of many waters: We thank Thee for the organ and the one whom Thou hast endowed with ability to play upon it. Guide her (him) to appropriate selections that will honor Thee; bless her (him) with a spirit of reverence and an alertness in mind. Direct her (his) fingers to notes and chords that will swell to praise Thee and Thy Son Jesus Christ, in whom is perfect concord. *Amen.*

2

O Thou who dost unlock the doors of the soul through the medium of music, and who speaks courage and peace to our hearts through songs: Bless with Thy spirit the voices of those who sing Thy message. Make Thy light to shine from their faces and Thy love to glow within their hearts, so that all who worship here may see the beauty of Thy holiness through Jesus Christ, our Lord.

Open Thou our lips, O Lord, and our mouths shall sing forth Thy praise. Attune our hearts unto Thee that we might worship Thee in spirit and in truth. *Amen.*

USHERS

For the privilege of service in this sacred and holy place, we pause to thank Thee. Help us now to be reverent in spirit and attentive to our task. Give to us an understanding of the holiness of worship and make us sensitive to the needs of Thy people. Guard us from disrespectful actions and from wandering thoughts. May all that we do be acceptable to Thee, through Jesus Christ our Lord. *Amen.*

THOSE RECEIVING THE OFFERING

1

As we receive and present to Thee the tithes and offerings of Thy children, grant that our own bodies, souls, minds, and spirits may be for Thee living sacrifices, holy and acceptable in Thy sight, through Jesus Christ our Lord. *Amen.*

2

O Lord, who art constantly adored, grant us an appreciative spirit, a dignified manner, a quiet confidence, and a sense of sacredness as we bring to Thine altar in behalf of these people their gifts of love and symbols of consecration, for Jesus' sake. *Amen.*

FOR THOSE CONDUCTING THE LORD'S SUPPER

Forbid us, O Lord, to take lightly this responsibility. As we handle these emblems representing our Saviour's broken body and shed blood, make us aware that this is holy ground. May nothing in our attitude, manner, or procedure interfere with the worshipers discerning the values unseen. As we assist others in their Holy Communion, may we likewise commune with Thee in spirit and in truth, through Jesus Christ our Lord. *Amen.*

For Others in the Community

FOR ATHLETIC HEROES

Today we want to pray for the athletic heroes. How they thrill us! We include the ones who can hit the home run that wins a tie game; the quarterback who can throw the winning touchdown pass with only seconds left to play; and the basketball wizard, whose skillful shooting brings victory as the buzzer sounds.

Lord, we spectators go wild over their feats. Thousands pay big money to watch their performance. Newspapers banner their names and carry their pictures; the pros offer fabulous sums; TV brings them into nearly every living room. Autograph seekers of all ages crowd upon them. Many with ulterior motives strive to manipulate and use them.

God, it must be difficult for athletes to keep humility, so we pray that these idols of our age may not think of themselves more highly than they ought to think.

Make them know that those whose names are in the headlines carry heavy responsibility; that those who are worshiped, must be worthy of adulation. For the sake of those whom they influence, help all athletes to be clean in speech, pure in motive, self-controlled, unselfish in attitude, and unashamedly committed to Christ and His Church.

Thus, may they and those whom they influence be equipped for the noble task of living, in the purpose of Jesus Christ. *Amen.*

FOR PHYSICIANS AND NURSES

We are especially appreciative, Father of compassion and healing, of those who care for the sick and afflicted. Grant to the physicians, not only wisdom and skill to diagnose and prescribe with accuracy, but the warmth and compassion that will reflect Your love to encourage the healing process. Save them from being impersonal, cold, and calculating. Diminish greed with unselfish service that loses self in love for persons. Sustain the physicians in health for their long and ever-demanding hours of work.

We take our hats off to the vigilant nurses who work in such close proximity to the ill, in all kinds of conditions and moods. Provide them with understanding, kindness, goodwill, patience, and spiritual commitment.

May the medicines remove the obstacles to health so that the marvelous recuperative powers may prevail and wholeness in body, mind, and spirit may eventuate. *Amen.*

FOR SCHOOLTEACHERS, ADMINISTRATORS, AND BOARD MEMBERS

Lord, these schoolteachers, administrators, and school board members deserve help. God, they have gone through extreme difficulties with the rebellious students, the integration transition, the emotional upheaval of parents, the controversies in curriculum, the pressures of unions, and even the takeover by militants.

Grant them, O Lord, patient cool in face of the defiant and rude. Help the teachers to be authoritative by a thorough grasp of their subjects, without the authority of the badge or stick. May their discipline be mature, consistent, and demanding, exercised with love and fairness. May the teachers be supported by wise and courageous administrators; may the administrators be supported by knowledgeable and principled board members; may the school boards be supported by an informed constituency, which knows the issues of the day, the values of balanced education, and provide adequately to meet the demands of a changing world. Thus, may the students learn that which is worth knowing, and love that worthy of their affections, for the health of our nation and world. *Amen.*

FOR THOSE STRIVING FOR A BETTER WORLD

O God, we pray your special blessings upon all people who are striving to make this a better world, especially: from the insincere, selfish, haughty, and publicity-minded. Help our leaders not to overreact until all challenges are silenced by the power of force and jail.

We remember long ago three men who died on Calvary—two because they were too bad; One because He was too good. Two were killed because they were below the level of society; One because He was above, disturbing and challenging the status quo. The gullible public crucified not only their sinners but also their Saviour. Forbid that we should do as they did. *Amen.*

LITANIES

1

LEADER We may die the death of a martyr and spill our blood as a symbol of honor for generations unborn;

PEOPLE But devoid of love, all these mean nothing, O Lord.

LEADER O Father, we must come to see that a man may be self-centered in his self-denial and self-righteous in his self-sacrifice; our generosity may feed our ego and our piety our pride.

PEOPLE Without love, benevolence becomes egotism and martyrdom becomes spiritual pride.

LEADER But the greatest of all virtues is love.

PEOPLE In a world dependent upon force, coercive tyranny, and bloody violence, we are challenged by your loving Son to follow in His love.

LEADER And then discover that unarmed love is the most powerful force in the world.

PEOPLE *Amen.* So be it.

JACK W. LUNDIN[4]

2

LITANY ON HUNGER FOR COMMUNITY

MINISTER We Thy gathered people, who often pretend to be so full of all spiritual truth, who exhalting ourselves look with disdain upon those who have not heard of our goodness, inwardly we acknowledge our emptiness before Thee, O God.

CONGREGATION Renew Thy Church, we beseech Thee.

MINISTER We who boast of our attendance at prayer breakfasts, family-night dinners, pie suppers, youth snacks, mission luncheons;

CONGREGATION We acknowledge our hunger for the reality of the Church, for Christ the Living Word.

MINISTER We who try to manipulate fellowship into existence and pretend to possess it in our phony forms of community;

CONGREGATION Grant us the gift of genuine community. Deliver us from the illusion that we can create Christian fellowship without Thy Living Word in our midst, or that we can program the Church into existence.

3

LITANY ON STEWARDSHIP

LEADER What shall it profit a man to gain the whole world if in the gaining he loses his own soul? What shall it profit a man to become president of his company—

RESPONSE —if he has no time left for his family?

LEADER What shall it profit a woman to serve on committees galore—

RESPONSE —if in the process she widens the generation gap at home?

LEADER   What shall it profit a young woman to be the most popular girl in her school—

RESPONSE   —if in the process she sacrifices her personal integrity?

LEADER   What shall it profit a young man to be a star athlete—

RESPONSE   —if along the way he is defeated by drugs?

LEADER   What shall it profit a man or woman, or boy or girl, to gain the whole world and lose his own soul?

SAMUEL F. PUGH

4

LITANY OF THE LORD'S PRAYER

LEADER   I cannot say . . .
"Our"

RESPONSE   if my religion has no room for other people and their needs.

LEADER   I cannot say . . .
"Father"

RESPONSE   if I do not demonstrate this relationship in my daily life.

LEADER   I cannot say . . .
"Who art in Heaven"

RESPONSE   if all my interests and pursuits are earthly things.

LEADER   I cannot say . . .
"Hallowed be Thy name"

RESPONSE   if I who am called by His name, am not holy.

LEADER   I cannot say . . .
"Thy Kingdom come"

RESPONSE   if I am unwilling to give up my sovereignty and accept the reign of God.

LEADER   I cannot say . . .
"Thy will be done"

RESPONSE   if I am unwilling or resentful of having Him in my life.

LEADER   I cannot say . . .
"On earth as it is in Heaven"

RESPONSE   unless I am truly ready to give myself to His service here and now.

LEADER   I cannot say . . .
"Give us this day our daily bread"

RESPONSE   without expending honest effort for it or by ignor-
ing the needs of my fellowmen.

LEADER   I cannot say . . .
"Forgive us our debts as we forgive our debtors"

RESPONSE   if I continue to harbor a grudge against anyone.

LEADER   I cannot say . . .
"Lead us not into temptation"

RESPONSE   if I deliberately choose to remain in a situation
where I am likely to be tempted.

LEADER   I cannot say . . .
"Deliver us from Evil"

RESPONSE   if I am not prepared to fight in the spiritual realm
with the weapon of prayer.

LEADER   I cannot say . . .
"Thine is the Kingdom, the Power, the Glory"

RESPONSE   if I do not give disciplined obedience,
if I fear what neighbors and friends may say or do,
if I seek my own glory first.

LEADER   I cannot say . . .
"Amen"

RESPONSE   unless I can honestly say also,
"Cost what it may, this is my prayer!"[5]

5

LITANY OF PRAYER

LEADER   Jesus said, ". . . when you pray, go into your room
. . . and pray to your Father who is in secret; and your Father
who sees in secret will reward you" (Matthew 6:6).

RESPONSE   O God, make your presence real and personal to
us now, as we withdraw in reverent conversation with You.

LEADER   Jesus said, "Ask, and it will be given you; seek, and
you will find; knock, and it will be opened to you" (7:7).

RESPONSE   O God, grant us persistence in our praying.

LEADER   Jesus said, "Do not fear, only believe" (Luke 8:50).

RESPONSE   O God, remove our doubts and dispel our fears with faith.

LEADER   Jesus said, "Watch and pray, that you may not enter into temptation" (Mark 14:38).

RESPONSE   O God, use our prayers to redirect and to restrain us.

LEADER   Jesus said, ". . . seek first his kingdom and his righteousness" (Matthew 6:33).

RESPONSE   O God, save us from selfish pleas and make your kingdom the content of our prayers.

LEADER   Jesus said, "Love your enemies, and pray for those who persecute you" (6:44).

RESPONSE   O God, incline our hearts to active concern and goodwill for those we do not understand and may our prayers soften the resentment and bridge the gaps.

UNISON   Jesus said, "Pray then like this:
Our Father in heaven:
Holy be your name,
Your kingdom come,
Your will be done,
    on earth as in heaven.
Give us today our daily bread,
Forgive us our sins,
    as we forgive those who sin against us.
Save us in the time of trial,
    and deliver us from evil.
For yours is the kingdom, the power, and
    the glory forever. *Amen*" (Paraphrased from Matthew 6:9–13).

INSPIRATIONAL MATERIALS

1

PSALM 1

Happy is that person who does not take advice from questionable sources; who does not keep company with the disreputable or join with malicious scoffers.

Rather, happy is the person who finds his satisfaction and joy in the Lord. He studies and meditates upon God's will for the day and for the night.

That person shall have deep roots like the tree, which reaches down into running streams of water. Such a tree is always alive, beautifully green, and blossoms with fruit at the proper season. So is the deeply rooted person, and men shall know him by his good works.

However, the wicked have no roots, hence no stability or good works. So, like fallen leaves, they are blown hither and yon by the prevailing wind.

The evil-intentioned person will not be able to hold up in the time of trial, nor be respected or approved in the company of the righteous.

God will vindicate the ways of righteousness, but the ways of evil ultimately will be frustrated and fade from sight.

2

PSALM 23

The Lord is my friend!
What more could I want?
He sits with me in the quiet times of my days.
He explores with me the meanings of life.
He calls me forth as a whole person.
Even though I walk along paths of pain, prejudice, hatred, depression,
My fears are quieted
Because He is with me.
His words and His thoughts,
They challenge me.
He causes me to be sensitive to the needs of mankind,
Then lifts up opportunities for serving.
His confidence stretches me.
Surely love shall be mine to share throughout my life,
And I shall be sustained by His concern forever.

JACQUIE CLINGAN

3

MATTHEW 25:35-46

I was hungry, and you formed a humanities club and discussed my hunger. Thank you.

I was imprisoned, and you crept off quietly to your chapel in the cellar and prayed for my release.

I was naked, and in your mind you debated the morality of my appearance.

I was sick, and you knelt and thanked God for your health.

I was homeless, and you preached to me of the spiritual shelter of the love of God.

I was lonely, and you left me alone to pray for me.

> You seem so holy; so close to God.
> But I'm still very hungry, and lonely, and cold.
> So where have your prayers gone?
> What have they done?
> What does it profit a man to page through his book of prayers when the rest of the world is crying for help?

AUTHOR UNKNOWN

4

ROMANS 12

Because of God's goodness to you, Christian friends, I urge you to use your bodies in dedicated service which God approves. Do not allow the patterns of secular people to mold you into their ways, but be different by the inner conditioning of your thoughts. Only then can you demonstrate unquestionable behavior and what is the true will of God.

Since we are all recipients of undeserved love and are, in a sense, dependent upon God's mercy, let no person have an exaggerated opinion of himself. Rather let him have confidence in his personal value because of the evidence of worth by God's love.

The human body has many parts, and each has its unique function, performing in intricate coordination with all other parts. The Church is like a body for doing Christ's will. We as parts of Christ's Body are united in Him. Each has a unique function to perform, depending upon his particular abilities given of God.

If you have ability to analyze and predict the future, do so with positive faith. If you have abilities to teach or counsel, to preach or lead, do so with concentration. If you are blessed with material wealth, be a liberal giver. If you have the ability to comfort and heal and to be compassionate, do so with joy.

Let your love be true. Cling tenaciously to what is good, while refusing absolutely all evil. In relationships with others, show tender concern; be warm-spirited and respectful; continue to pray regularly; keep communications open, especially with the godly, and be hospitable. Share the joy of those who are joyful, and enter vicariously into the sorrow of those who weep.

Have the same attitude toward everyone. Do not feel aloof and superior to lowly tasks or common people or things as though you were conceited. Give attention to what is honorable. Seek no retaliation when unjustly abused, for vengeance belongs to God alone. Let Him punish and you can be sure He will. So far as your actions are concerned, be peaceful with all men. If an offender is hungry or thirsty, arrange food for him; this will soften his feelings toward you. In this way enemies may be turned into friends. So, be careful not to be overcome by evil. You overcome evil by doing good.

5

1 CORINTHIANS 12:12–13:13

Just as a team is a unit but has many players and all the players on the team—even though there are many of them—make up one team, so it is with Christ. For by one Spirit we all were selected for this squad—whether American or European, Caucasian or Negro—and all have been inspired by the one Spirit.

For the team does not consist of one player, but of many. If the guard should say, "Because I am not an end, I do not belong to the team," that would not make him any less a member of the team.

If the outfielder should say, "Because I am not a pitcher, I do not belong to the team," he would still be a necessary member of the team. If the whole team were pitchers, who would cover third? If the whole team were halfbacks, who would snap the ball? But as it is, God has arranged positions on the team according to the rules of the game. If everybody played the same position, where would the team be? So there are many positions but only one team. The quarterback cannot say to the tackle, "Who needs you?" Nor the forward to the guard, "Get lost." On the contrary, the positions which may seem to be inconspicuous may really be indispensable.

Now you are a team for Christ. Each of you is a team member. And God has assigned different positions to be played. So you are certainly wise to desire the finest skills.

I will show you a more excellent way. If I can play many sports but have not love, I am merely a flashy player. If I know all about athletics, and have the skill to become a coach, but have not love, I am just a nobody. If I really give all I've got to being an outstanding player, and have not love, my score is zero.

Then what is love? Love is a combination of many attitudes, like patience, kindness, like considering the other person's point of view, like not being glad when somebody drops out, but being glad when he makes good.

There are three basic skills for living: faith, hope, and love. But the greatest of these is love.[6]

6

A PARAPHRASE OF 1 CORINTHIANS 13

If I can sing "Green Grow the Rushes Ho" from memory or preach like Billy Graham, but say nothing loving, I am nothing but an untuned electric guitar or a set of drums. If I have ESP and am learned as Einstein, or can blow up Fort Knox by the exertion of faith alone, but have no love in my heart, I am as empty as outer space. If I put my whole wardrobe in the Goodwill Box, or set myself afire like a Buddhist monk, but do them without love, I accomplish exactly zero.

Love does not lose its cool. It is thoughtful of others' feelings. Love is not a green-eyed monster. Love is not snobbish and forms no cliques. It is not rude, crude, and unattractive. It does not insist on its own way like Lucy does in "Peanuts." Love is not like parents before they've had their morning coffee. Love does not feel the same way I do when a teacher asks a question on the final that has never been discussed in class. Love does not spread gossip but instead is glad to have it squashed. Love trusts in the strength and righteousness of God. It sees the doughnut and not the hole. Love puts up with small irritations constantly.

Love is for keeps. As for Ouija boards and political speeches and Ph.D.s, they will croak. Our data is incomplete, and tea leaves sometimes lie. But when love reigns, war and hunger and strife will end. When I was a kid, I talked baby talk, my thoughts were immature, my reasoning for the birds. But when I grew up, I began to mature. As long as we are trapped inside these human bodies, we can only partially understand the wonders of the universe, but one day God's knowledge will be ours, and we will know Him as completely as He knows us. So faith, hope and love will last forever, but I'll put my money on love.

7

The love in church community means that we ought to take one another on for better or for worse, for always. And a member who continues long in sickness or disability will test the Church to the uttermost. To undertake intercession for a sick man, we have to see the family through a difficult time. We may have to see the man's widow and children through their adjustment to life after his death—not just spiritually, but materially too. Every member of the congregation will be the better or the worse for accepting or refusing responsibility. Intercession will not merely *demand* this of us, but will *do* this to us.

DANIEL JENKINS[7]

8

While women weep as they do now, I'll fight; while little children go hungry as they do now, I'll fight; while men go to prison, in and out, in and out, I'll fight; while there is a poor, lost girl upon the street, I'll fight; while there yet remains one dark soul without the light of God, I'll fight—I'll fight to the very end.

GENERAL WILLIAM BOOTH
Salvation Army

9

BEATITUDES OF THE AGED

1. Blessed are they who understand my faltering step and palsy hand.
2. Blessed are they who know my ears today must strain to catch the things they say.
3. Blessed are they who seem to know that my eyes are dim and my wits slow.
4. Blessed are they with a cheery smile who stop to chat for a little while.
5. Blessed are they who never say, "You have told that story twice today."
6. Blessed are they who make it known that I am respected, loved, and not alone.
7. Blessed are they who know the way to bring back memories of yesterday.
8. Blessed are they who make it known that I am at a loss for strength to carry the cross.
9. Blessed are they who ease the days on my journey home in loving ways.

10

THE MINISTER'S IF

If you can keep your faith when those about you
    are wrestling with theirs, and blame their doubts on you;
If you can trust in God when all men doubt Him,
    yet make allowance for that doubting too.

If you can serve and not get tired of serving,
    or facing critics, look with loving eyes;
Or being slandered, still be understanding,
    and yet don't act too proud that you are wise.
If you can keep your eyes upon the Master,
    keep serving Him your fundamental aim;
If you can meet with crowded pews or vacant,
    yet preach your best each Sunday just the same.
If you can bear to see the flock you've pastored
    split by an elder stubborn as a mule,
And patch the pieces back into Christ's Body
    with love that even seeks to love the fool!
If you can make a heap of your possessions
    and follow where you hear the Spirit's call;
Take name and fame and earth's success and fortune,
    and make the risen Saviour Lord of all.
If you can force faint faith and flagging spirit
    to serve God's will long after they are weak;
And so serve on when there is nothing in you
    except the grace of Him for whom you speak.
If you can preach to crowds and be prophetic,
    or be profound, and keep the common touch,
God's truth and love the only lights that guide you
    and praise from men not valued overmuch.
If you can live your life in faithful service,
    the way of Christ the only path you choose,
You'll be the type of man God often blesses,
    but what is more, you'll be a man He'll use!
—A Minister of Good News!

JAMES PEYTON HOPKINS[8]

OFFERTORY SENTENCES AND PRAYERS

1

Honor and majesty are before him; strength and beauty are in his sanctuary. Ascribe to the Lord, O families of the peoples, ascribe to the Lord glory and strength! Ascribe to the Lord the glory due his name; bring an offering, and come into his courts (Psalms 96:6–8).

O Lord, Thou has blessed us far beyond our deserving or ability to understand. We present now, in humility and thankfulness, our tokens of gratitude for Thy tender mercies, and dedicate them to Thy Kingdom's work, through Jesus Christ our Lord. *Amen.*

2

Bring the full tithes into the storehouse, that there may be food in my house; and thereby put me to the test, says the Lord of hosts, if I will not open the windows of heaven for you and pour down for you an overflowing blessing (Malachi 3:10).

O Lord, who hast redeemed us with a costly sacrifice of blood: May we not offer Thee the leftover of Thy bounty to us, but rather a sacred portion in respect to Thine ownership of all and to demonstrate our earnestness for the sake of Jesus Christ. *Amen.*

3

And he said to them, "Go into all the world and preach the gospel to the whole creation. He who believes and is baptized will be saved; but he who does not believe will be condemned" (Mark 16:15, 16).

God and Father of mankind, who dost have the ultimate claim upon our lives, illumine us with the significance of the Great Commission, compel us with the urgency of the task, and grant us the dedication to do our part in spreading Thy Gospel over all the earth, to the end that men, everywhere, may know Thee through Jesus Christ. *Amen.*

4

And he said to all, "If any man would come after me, let him deny himself and take up his cross daily and follow me" (Luke 9:23).

Forbid, O God, that we should forget, amid our earthly comforts, the pains of betrayal, lonely agony, false accusations, broken heart, and torturous death that our Lord Jesus endured for our salvation. As Thou didst give Thyself utterly for us, may we give ourselves entirely to Thee. *Amen.*

5

You give but little when you give of your possessions. It is when you give of yourself that you truly give.

6

Lord, I've been given
    eyes to see,
    ears to hear,
    hands to hold,
    feet to run,
But what have I given thee?
Lord, I've shared
    skies and seas,
    fields and grains,
    sun and stars,
    fruits and flowers,
But what have I given thee?
Lord, the days were long,
And the years were lean,
And I've known despair;
But, through it all,
I've breathed a prayer:
"Lord, as I live, let me give,
    And in the season's ending,
    Let me affirm
    My joy was not in spending,
        saving,
        receiving,
        talking,
        holding,
But in the act of giving!"

CHRISTOPHER T. GARRIOTT

7

O God, remembering our accountability to You for the use we make of time, talent, and money, we present our offerings, praying that they might reflect responsible stewardship, and be acceptable in Christ's Spirit. *Amen.*

8

Not of our deserving, but of Thy kind Providence, O God, have we been blessed with affluence and opportunity. Grant us humble gratitude and a spirit of compelling generosity, knowing that to whom much is given, from him much is required, in Jesus' Spirit. *Amen.*

9

SEE THIS BILL?

Lord, you know this bill's history and its secrets. It has passed through many hands

—of persons who have knocked themselves out to possess it for a few hours;

—of persons who have sacrificed honor and conscience, to have through it a little pleasure, a little joy.

Oh, what stories this bill can tell from its long, silent journey: "I have purchased bread for the family table. I have bought corsages and gifts of affection for young lovers. I have paid for a wedding ceremony. I have brought laughter to the young, and joy to the elders. I have bought books to inform the mind of all ages. I have paid for medicines and physicians to save the sick. I have been given to clothe and feed the unfortunate. I have been given to honor God's ownership, and support the church's ministry.

"But also I have bought liquor that has debased human potential. I have produced movies unfit to be shown to children and have recorded indecent songs. I have paid for human blood, and broken the morals of adolescence. I have been used to print pornography and to purchase the body of a woman for a few minutes. I have paid for the weapons of crime and war."

Lord, I thank You for all the joy and life this bill has brought. I ask Your forgiveness for all the evil it has made possible. I offer it now as a symbol of my gratitude, and my convictions, and dedicate it to Your spiritual purposes as known in Jesus Christ.

10

THE AGONY OF GOD

I listen to the agony of God—
 I who am fed,
 Who never yet went hungry for a day.
 I see the dead—
 The children starved for lack of bread—
 I see, and try to pray.

I listen to the agony of God—
 I who am warm,
 Who never yet have lacked a sheltering home.
 In dull alarm
 The dispossessed of hut and farm,
 Aimless and "transient" roam.

I listen to the agony of God—
 I who am strong,
 With health, and love, and laughter in my soul.
 I see a throng
 Of stunted children reared in wrong,
 And wish to make them whole.

  I listen to the agony of God—
   But know full well
   That not until I share their bitter cry—
   Earth's pain and hell—
   Can God within my spirit dwell
   To bring His Kingdom nigh.

GEORGIA HARKNESS[9]

BENEDICTIONS AND DISMISSALS

1

The Lord bless you and keep you: The Lord make his face to shine upon you, and be gracious to you: The Lord lift up his countenance upon you, and give you peace. *Amen* (Numbers 6:24–26).

2

Grace [be] to you and peace from God our Father and the Lord Jesus Christ (1 Corinthians 1:3).

3

And the peace of God, which passes all understanding, will keep your hearts and your minds in Christ Jesus (Philippians 4:7).

4

The grace of the Lord Jesus Christ and the love of God and the fellowship of the Holy Spirit be with you all (2 Corinthians 13:14).

5

Now to him who by the power at work within us is able to do far more abundantly than all that we ask or think, to him be glory in the church and in Christ Jesus to all generations, for ever and ever. *Amen* (Ephesians 3:20, 21).

6

Now to him who is able to keep you from falling and to present you without blemish before the presence of his glory with rejoicing, to the only God, our Savior through Jesus Christ our Lord, be glory, majesty, dominion, and authority, before all time and now and for ever. *Amen* (Jude 1:24, 25).

7

Spirit of Jesus, present now within our hearts; we are thankful for the sacraments of which we have eaten and drunk to remember our Lord's death and taste His living presence; for all the earthly symbols by which unseen realities have a firmer hold upon our souls; for the music which has inspired us, the fellowship that has encouraged us, and the interior peace that has quieted us. Grant, our Heavenly Father, that the spiritual refreshment we have experienced may strengthen us in our Christian witness to honor Christ's love and spirit. *Amen.*

8

Divine Parent, let Thy highest blessings rest upon each of us and upon Your Church everywhere, now and forever more. *Amen.*

9

MINISTER   May the peace of God dwell in your hearts.
CHOIR (*in unison*)   Forever.
PERSON IN ONE SECTION   Forever.
ANOTHER PERSON IN ANOTHER SECTION   Forever.
ANOTHER PERSON IN ANOTHER SECTION   Forever.
MINISTER   So may it be.

10

MINISTER   The Lord bless you, everyone.
CONGREGATION (*shouting*)   **AMEN!**
MINISTER   The Lord is with you, everyone.
CONGREGATION (*whispering*)   Amen.
MINISTER   The Lord loves you, everyone.
CONGREGATION (*singing regular threefold Amen tune*)   Amen, Amen, Amen.

11

God sends you from the gathered Church, to be the scattered Church, let loose in a world that is resistant to Him. Into your varied occupations, may you make your world His world, a world that is "new in Christ." May God's Spirit go and abide with you. *Amen.*

12

We have met Jesus of Nazareth, and for that reason the concerns of the whole world are our concerns. In the prayers of this community, we go now from this place with the intention to live for others. The Lord be with you. Go. Serve in His name.

13

Go out into the world in peace;
   have courage; hold on to what is good;
   return no man evil for evil;
strengthen the fainthearted;
   support the weak;
help the suffering; honor all men;
   love the unloved;
serve the Lord; rejoicing in the power
of the Holy Spirit.

14

LEADER   Go in peace. You are forgiven.
Jesus Christ Himself has reconciled the past.
RESPONSE   So be it.
LEADER   Go also in service.
Remember those in prison, the poor, the anxious, the despairing, and those who fear death. Tell them by your life that they are loved and accepted.
RESPONSE   So be it.
LEADER   Go in trust.
We who wear the mantle of the finite are cared for through all eternity.
RESPONSE   Thanks to be God. *Amen and amen.*

Section 2

THE COMMUNION OF
THE LORD'S SUPPER

Celebrating Communion

Invitations and Meditations

Communion Prayers

Words of Institution

Candlelight Communion

CELEBRATING COMMUNION

What if the world should forget Jesus? What if the meaning of His death should fade from Christian understanding? What if His forgiveness, presence, and victory should vanish from our consciousness? Hope would vanish. Sin would abound. Sacrifice for good would cease. The redemptive community would disperse.

That is why Jesus instituted a single yet solemn ordinance, saying, "Do this in remembrance of Me." The Holy Communion has become the dearest experience on earth for the Christian, for there we sense Christ's presence, reality, sacrifice, and living Body.

While frequency of the service, methods of participation, and theological understanding vary, nevertheless, the Holy Communion is a very special and sacred occasion for all serious Christians. All should approach it with prayerful dignity and spiritual preparation.

It has been so from the early beginning as Luke records. "And they [the disciples] devoted themselves to . . . breaking of bread . . ." (Acts 2:42). "On the first day of the week, when we were gathered together to break bread . . ." (20:7). It holds a central place in our Christian worship.

INVITATIONS AND MEDITATIONS

1

"I am the living bread which came down from heaven; if any one eats of this bread, he will live for ever; and the bread which

I shall give for the life of the world is my flesh." . . . So Jesus said to them, "Truly, truly, I say to you, unless you eat the flesh of the Son of Man and drink his blood, you have no life in you; he who eats my flesh and drinks my blood has eternal life, and I will raise him up at the last day. For my flesh is food indeed, and my blood is drink indeed. He who eats my flesh and drinks my blood abides in me, and I in him" (John 6:51, 53–56).

2

For just as the body is one and has many members, and all the members of the body, though many, are one body, so it is with Christ. For by one Spirit we were all baptized into one body—Jews or Greeks, slaves or free—and all were made to drink of one Spirit. . . . Now you are the body of Christ and individually members of it (1 Corinthians 12:12, 13, 27).

3

On the first day of the week . . . we were gathered together to break bread. . . . And they devoted themselves to the apostles' teaching and fellowship, to the breaking of bread and the prayers (Acts 20:7; 2:42).

4

Greater love has no man than this, that a man lay down his life for his friends. . . . But God shows his love for us in that while we were yet sinners Christ died for us (John 15:13; Romans 5:8).

5

Come to this table, not because you must but because you may; come to testify not that you are righteous but that you sincerely love our Lord Jesus Christ and desire to be His true disciples. Come, not because you are strong, but because you are weak; not because you have any claim on heaven's rewards, but because in your frailty and sin you stand in constant need of heaven's mercy and help; come, not to express an opinion, but to seek a Presence and to pray for a Spirit. And now that the Supper of the Lord is spread before you, lift up your minds and hearts above all selfish fears and cares. Let this bread and this cup be to you the witness and signs of the grace of our Lord Jesus Christ, the love of God, and the communion of the Holy Spirit. Before the throne of the Heavenly Father and the cross of the Redeemer make your humble confession of sin, consecrate your lives to Christian obedience and service, and pray for strength to do the holy and blessed will of God.

AUTHOR UNKNOWN

6

THE ART OF REMEMBERING

Do this in remembrance of me (1 Corinthians 11:24).

Memory is a balancing factor in life. Though we are not to live *in* the past, we do live *by* the past. We keep photographs, mementos, and symbols to remind us of important events, sacrifices made for our heritage, vows we have made, and the love we cherish.

Our Lord did not want to be forgotten. He knew that if faith, morality, love, and proper motivation were to be kept alive in His disciples, they must remember the purity of His life, the cost of His sacrifice, and the power of the Resurrection.

So we come to this table today, remembering that here we may come as near to Calvary as man may come ... remembering the "Lamb of God that taketh away the sin of the world" ... remembering the great cloud of witnesses all of whose hands have been on the table and who have since gone to the "place of many mansions" ... remembering what we are and what we can become in Christ ... remembering that we live not so much to be loved as to love, not to be served but to serve.

7

LORD, IS IT I?

When it was evening, he sat at table with the twelve disciples; and as they were eating, he said, "Truly, I say to you, one of you will betray me." And they were very sorrowful, and began to say to him one after another, "Is it I, Lord?" (Matthew 26:20–22).

The saddest event recorded in Scripture is not what happened on a hill outside of Jerusalem; it is what happened in the Upper Room. The saddest words of the Bible are not "and they crucified him," but these: "One of you shall betray me." The cruelest nails ever driven were not those driven into the hands and feet of Jesus, but those His friends drove into His heart.

When the will of Jesus went contrary to the desire of one of the disciples, he betrayed the Lord for a few worldly coins. When following Jesus became dangerous, and when He needed loyal support, His disciples forsook Him and fled. When an opportunity was given to testify, one who followed afar off denied Him three times.

It still goes on among His most trusted followers. The Upper Room question is still appropriate for us to ask in these quiet moments of introspection. "Lord, is it I?"

8

Friends, if you sincerely want to turn your back on your sins, if you wish to be transformed from a patronizing member to an involved disciple, and desire to lead a new life of love and compassion, then get ready to come to God in faith, confident of His forgiveness.

9

Welcome to the celebration. You are invited here to celebrate what the early Christians celebrated in the Eucharist feast—Jesus Christ—His life, His love, His words, His joy, His triumph over death. Let us shout the joy of our hope—and celebrate!

10

The Lord's Supper is a memorial to the sacrifice of our Lord for the sins of men, a means of grace to those who believe in

Him, a bond and pledge of union with Him, and with each other in His mystical body.

Therefore, it is necessary that we come to this table with understanding, faith, repentance, and love, not holding fellowship with evil, or cherishing self-righteousness, but conscious of our weakness and in sorrow for our sins, humbly putting our trust in Christ, and seeking His grace.

Draw near then, to the Holy Table, and hear the words of the Lord Jesus Christ: "Come to me, all who labor and are heavy laden, and I will give you rest." (Adapted from the Book of Common Order of the Church of Scotland.)

11

NOT BY BREAD ALONE

Man does not live by bread alone, but by beauty and harmony, truth and goodness, work and recreation, affection and friendship, aspiration and worship.

Not by bread alone, but by the splendor of the firmament at night, the glory of the heavens at dawn, the blending of colors at sunset, the loveliness of magnolia trees, the magnificence of mountains.

Not by bread alone, but by the majesty of ocean breakers, the shimmer of moonlight on a calm lake, the flashing silver of a mountain torrent, the exquisite patterns of snow crystals, the creations of artists.

Not by bread alone, but by the sweet song of a mockingbird, the rustle of the wind in the trees, the magic of a violin, the sublimity of a softly lighted cathedral.

Not by bread alone, but by the fragrance of roses, the scent of orange blossoms, the smell of new-mown hay, the clasp of a friend's hand, the tenderness of a mother's kiss.

Not by bread alone, but by the lyrics of poets, the wisdom of sages, the holiness of saints, the biographies of great souls.

Not by bread alone, but by comradeship and high adventure, seeking and finding, serving and sharing, loving and being loved.

Man does not live by bread alone, but by being faithful in prayer, responding to the guidance of the Holy Spirit, finding and doing the loving will of God now and eternally.

12

WHY I COME TO THE LORD'S TABLE

I come not because I am worthy, not for any righteousness of mine. For I have sinned and fallen short of what, by God's help, I might have been.

But, I come because Christ bids me come. It is His table. And He invites me.

I come because it is a memorial to Him, as oft it is done in remembrance of Him. And when I remember Him—His life, His sufferings and death, I find myself humbling myself in His presence and bowing in worship.

I come, because here is portrayed Christian self-denial, and I am taught very forcibly the virtue of sacrifice on behalf of another which has salvation in it.

I come, because here I have the opportunity to acknowledge my unworthiness and to make a new start.

I come, because here I find comfort and peace.

I come, because here I find hope.

I come, because I rise from this place with new strength, courage, and power to live for Him who died for me.

COMMUNION PRAYERS

1

PRAYER OF CONFESSION

O God, whose mercy is everlasting; we confess that we have been unworthy of Thy sacrifice in Christ. We have dishonored Thy name by our carelessness in word and deed. We remember promises that we have failed to keep. We have fashioned excuses to hide our faltering loyalty. We approach Thee, not through any merit of our own, but through Jesus Christ, Thy Son, our Savior, who lived and died for our salvation. As we eat and drink these emblems, forgive us, O Lord. Perfect Thy strength in our weakness. Remind us, when our hearts condemn us, that Thy love is greater than our sins and can cleanse us from unrighteousness, now through Jesus Christ our Lord. *Amen.*

2

We thank Thee, our Heavenly Father, for this table to which we come, remembering our Lord whose body was broken and whose blood was shed that we may have life. Give us a new vision and a more perfect appreciation of Thine infinite love and mercy. Let these emblems speak to us of redemption from sin and of life eternal which we know through Him, whose life, death, and Resurrection are represented here. Help us to forget the lesser things that so engross us and help us to fix our attention on that quality of life which is eternal. Give us strength to face temptation, courage to meet any evil that may beset us, and forgiveness for our failures, in Jesus' name. *Amen.*

3

Merciful Father, we Thy children assemble in Thy name and in Thy house to break bread and drink of the cup in memory of Thy Son, our Saviour, Jesus Christ. Grant that we may have understanding and humility as we seek to reenact our Lord's Last Supper. Hear us as each in his own way seeks personal communion with Thee through Jesus Christ. *Amen.*[10]

4

Our Father, who hast been made known to us in Christ, we pray that we may feel Thy presence here today and that Thy Spirit and way of life may be real to us. We thank Thee for these emblems of our Lord's broken body and shed blood, which remind us that He gave His life that we may see in Him Thy love for us. Help us to know that in Thy love we have grace and mercy through which all our repented sins are forgiven, and by which our lives may be transformed with newness. We come before Thee, remembering that even as Thou dost love and forgive us, so ought we to love and forgive one another. Strengthen our faith in Christ and help us to be consecrated to His way. *Amen.*

5

O God, who canst guide our feet into the sanctuary of Thy presence: Make ready, we beseech Thee, our hearts to receive the sacrament of that love whereby Thy Son hath redeemed us. *Amen.*

6

We do not come to this table, O Lord, counting on our own goodness. For we know that we have missed the mark of our high calling. We trust in Your love. Help us to receive this sacrament as a gift from You of forgiveness, of a new chance at life, of strength for our spirits, as hope for our tomorrows. May we grow to be like You, as You become the center of our living. *Amen.*

7

Giver of our daily bread, help us to know that You are our very Bread of Life. Feed us spiritually, as we partake physically of the loaf which we ask You now to bless. As bread is the staff of life for our bodies, may You be the staff of our spiritual selves. Strengthen us for our work, and draw us ever to Yourself in love beyond our deserving. *Amen.*

SAMUEL F. PUGH

8

Father, it is at the table of Communion that we participate in the body of Christ.

We are grateful that we are "called to be one . . . in the Lord." Surely it is around this table that our oneness has its birth and its fulfillment.

We are not here because of status, standing, or capability. We have come to break the bread of reality. We eat the bread for our own fulfillment:

The fulfillment of transcendent love.
The fulfillment of spiritual healing.
The fulfillment of forgiveness.
The fulfillment of sacrificial service.
The fulfillment of becoming.
The fulfillment of oneness in our Lord.

Take us as we are and nurture us into more than we are through Holy Communion. This is our need. This is our prayer. *Amen.*

DR. KATHLEEN BAILEY AUSTIN

WORDS OF INSTITUTION

1

FOR THE BREAD   Now as they were eating, Jesus took bread and blessed, and broke it, and gave it to the disciples and said, "Take, eat; this is my body."

FOR THE CUP   And he took a cup, and when he had given thanks he gave it to them, saying, "Drink of it, all of you; for this is my blood of the covenant, which is poured out for many for the forgiveness of sins" (Matthew 26:27, 28).

2

FOR THE BREAD   The Lord Jesus on the night when he was betrayed took bread, and when he had given thanks, he broke it, and said, "This is my body which is for you. Do this in remembrance of me."

FOR THE CUP   . . . In the same way also the cup, after supper, saying, "This cup is the new covenant in my blood. Do this, as often as you drink it, in remembrance of me" (1 Corinthians 11:23–25).

3

FOR THE BREAD   As they were eating, Jesus took a small loaf of bread and blessed it and broke it apart and gave it to the disciples and said, "Take it and eat it, for this is my body" (Matthew 26:26, 27).

FOR THE CUP   And he took a cup of wine and gave thanks for

it and gave it to them and said, "Each one drink from it, for this is my blood, sealing the New Covenant. It is poured out to forgive the sins of multitudes" (vs. 28, 29).

4

FOR THE BREAD   This is what the Lord himself has said about his table, and I passed it on to you before: That on the night when Judas betrayed him, the Lord Jesus took bread. And when he had given thanks to God for it, he broke it and gave it to his disciples and said, "Take this and eat it. This is my body, which is given for you. Do this to remember me" (1 Corinthians 11:23, 24).

FOR THE CUP   In the same way, he took the cup of wine after supper, saying, "This cup is the new agreement between God and you that has been established and set in motion by my blood. Do this in remembrance of me whenever you drink it" (v. 25).

CANDLELIGHT COMMUNION

(This Candlelight Communion or Service of Darkness commemorates the suffering and death of Christ, and is based on the ancient Tenebrae. Dating from the eighth century, Tenebrae was originally celebrated on Wednesday, Thursday, and Friday of Holy Week. It represented the darkness that fell over the earth as the Son of God was crucified.

The seven anthems are designed where spoken meditations, based on the "Seven Words from the Cross," are given. With each meditation the candles are progressively extinguished. The glow from this last vigil candle indicates that death only seems to triumph over Christ, and points toward the coming Resurrection.

The communion service commemorates our Lord's Last Supper with His disciples before His death, and the prediction of His betrayal. Worshipers will be led to the communion table one row at a time for simultaneous partaking.

(Worshipers are requested to leave in silence and not talk until they are in their cars.)

Prelude Music

> Organ—"Pre'ambule" .... Vierne
> Carillon—"Come Sweet Death" .... Bach

(The sanctuary is turned to darkness. A seven-branch candelabrum and one central candle, representing Christ, are lit on the communion table. Then follows the silent CHOIR *processional.)*

HYMN   "Beneath the Cross of Jesus"

Invocation

O God, as we come here to remember the suffering and death of our Lord Jesus Christ, grant that we may remember that He was wounded for *our* transgressions; He was bruised for *our* iniquities. The chastisement of *our* peace was upon Him, and with His stripes we are healed. Grant that we may confess our share in the sins that crucified Him, and also be partakers in the reconciliation which He made possible. So may it be. *Amen.*

Introductory Meditation   "Jesus' Death Upon the Cross"

We come tonight to look at the cross, where Jesus was the victim of human injustice and wickedness. His arrest, trial, and death compose the greatest miscarriage of justice in all history. It was a struggle in which good and evil, principle and expediency, sacrifice and self-interest, adventuresome thinking and conservatism, love and hate met. Christ was the victim of these unworthy forces in the human heart that caused His painful death and for a while conquered Him, but from which in the end He arose to triumph over evil.

Let us look to see the Spirit of our Master, standing up before the world against all its brutality and sin. We see it in the Seven Words from the Cross.

I. The Darkness of Betrayal

MEDITATION   Hear the First Word: "Father, forgive these people" (*see* Luke 23:34).

In the first word, "Father, forgive these people, for they

don't know what they are doing," we see His magnanimous spirit, stooping to a generous gesture towards His persecutors in the midst of His agony. They knew so little about Him. It reveals to us the depth of His redemptive passion. It should cut in upon our complacent discipleship until we pray, "Father, forgive *us;* we know not what we do."

ANTHEM   "When Jesus Wept" (*extinguish the first light*)

II. The Darkness of Separation

MEDITATION   Hear the Second Word: "Today shalt thou be with me in paradise" (Luke 23:43 KJV).

The spirit of Jesus in His suffering—His compassion, His magnanimity, His faith—drew one of the men on an adjacent cross into His presence. Jesus made it possible for this thief to see the mercy of God and to believe in the compassion of God. In His characteristic compassion Jesus turned and said the second word from the cross, "Today, you will be with Me in paradise. This is a solemn promise." Paradise is open to those who, conscious of their sin and guilt, hunger after righteousness, and seek the mercy of God through Christ.

ANTHEM   "Verily, Thou Shalt Be" (*extinguish the second light*)

III. The Darkness of Crucifixion

MEDITATION   Hear the Third Word: "Woman, behold your son" (John 19:26).

The third word from the cross was, "Woman, behold your son! Behold your mother."

What compassionate thoughtfulness and tender care are in the midst of excruciating agony. His reasons were deeper than sentiment. Mary had never understood her Son. It was hard for her to be reconciled to the course He had taken. This was a terrible experience for a mother. Through this trying ordeal and years beyond, she would need understanding, and sustaining fellowship. It was, therefore, her spiritual welfare about which Jesus was concerned. That is why He commended her care to John, the beloved disciple.

ANTHEM   "This Is My Commandment" (*extinguish the third light*)

IV. The Darkness of Desertion

MEDITATION   Hear the Fourth Word: "My God, My God, why hast thou forsaken me?" (Matthew 27:46).

No more poignant words have ever wrung from human lips than these words that came from Jesus in the midst of the crucifixion torment and torture. "My God, My God, why have You forsaken Me?" Jesus suffered not only the terrible physical agony of a horrible, lingering death, but the greater torment of spiritual aloneness, a desperate feeling expressed in the Twenty-Second Psalm. All great men are truly lonely. Jesus was going in a direction no man had gone before, from which there was no turning back. For a moment how lonely and desperate He must have felt in this struggle against evil!

ANTHEM   "Lenten Prayer" (*extinguish the fourth light*)

V. The Darkness of Evil's Torture

MEDITATION   Hear the Fifth Word: "I thirst" (John 19:28).

"I'm thirsty" is the only word from the cross which refers to Jesus' physical suffering. How awful is the agony of thirst, especially in the hot, sweltering sun of Palestine; no part of His body was free from pain. The loss of blood, the mounting fever, the unnatural sag of His unsupported body, the nails scraping exposed nerves, the swollen wounds and raw bruises, and the nauseating odor of dripping blood brought forth this cry of His humanity, "I'm thirsty." His was a man's body. He endured the full measure of evil's torment and torture. God sought our salvation through a man, not an angel, or a seraph, but through One who belonged to us and suffered at our hands.

ANTHEM   "Were You There" (*extinguish the fifth light*)

VI. The Darkness of Complete Sacrifice

MEDITATION   Hear the Sixth Word: "It is finished" (John 19:30).

Finally, Jesus' power to endure pain was exhausted which brought to His lips the parting cry, "It is finished." To be sure, His agony, ordeal, and testing were finished. His mission, His earthly work, and life were finished. The long, painful path of duty and obedience to God's purpose, which He had followed so loyally, was terminated. He had fulfilled His mission. It was completed. The work He had been appointed to do was over. The cosmic struggle was through. Despite the suffering, love and faith were still alive in Him.

ANTHEM   "Go to Dark Gethsemane" (*extinguish the sixth light*)

VII. The Darkness of Death

MEDITATION   Hear the Seventh Word: "Father, I commit my spirit to you" (*see* Luke 23:46).

The last word, "Father, I commit my spirit to you," is the triumphant declaration of a confident faith, putting His complete loyalty in the hands of the Father. His entire life had been a venture in faith. Everything was at stake. He gave to God a completely loyal instrument. He had been tempted to abandon it. Often He had been assailed by doubts. Yet He prayed, "Not My will but Yours." He entrusted His life and His work and now His future to God's hands. This is the highest act of faith for the Christian, to do as did our Master, "Into Your hands I commit my life with all its suffering and defeats and broken purposes, to be used and perfected by You."

ANTHEM   "Through Him Alone" (*extinguish the seventh light*)

Communion in Darkness

COMMUNION MEDITATION (*only single candle on communion table remains lighted*)

Is it nothing to you, all you that pass by?

Sometimes it causes my heart to tremble, tremble, tremble—because the sins which put Him there cannot be dated. Stupidity, fear of truth and goodness, intolerance and prejudice, hate and jealousy, cruelty and compromise were there—and these are not dated. Calvary is eternally relevant as redemptive love and man's evil come into tension. Were you there—when Jesus predicted one would betray Him? Were you there—when they forsook Him and fled? Were you there—when they shouted, "Crucify Him!"? In a sense, we were all there, and we ask tonight, "Lord, is it I? Am I betraying You? Am I driving nails into Your body? Am I crucifying You anew?"

Not only once, and long ago,
There on Golgotha's side,
Has Christ, the Lord, been crucified
Because He loved a lost world so.
But hourly souls, sin-satisfied,
Mock His great love, flout His commands.
And I drive nails deep in His hands,
You thrust the spear within His side.

JOHN RICHARD MORELAND

Let everyone examine himself—and in the light of His forgiveness and victory, seek divine forgiveness, and renew your allegiance.

HYMN "Bread of the World, in Mercy Broken" (*one verse*)

COMMUNION PARTICIPATION (*one row at a time comes to the table*)

Silent Recessional

Section 3

THE MINISTRY TO THE SICK

A Caring Fellowship

Hospital Visitation

Prayers for the Sick

Appropriate Scripture Readings

Homebound Communion

Nursing Home Service

Communion to the Sick

A CARING FELLOWSHIP

In the Epistle of James we read, "Religion that is pure and undefiled before God . . . is this: to visit orphans and widows in their affliction . . ." (James 1:27). With the increased elderly population, the church's ministry to the homebound, sick, and troubled is expanded. There are increasing numbers of nursing homes and hospitals to accommodate this segment. It is incumbent upon the church to be a caring fellowship and to keep in touch with these people, rendering them a spiritual ministry. The minister is a significant part of the healing team. Following are materials designed to be used for individuals or for group service. (Minister will substitute proper pronoun *him/her* as is appropriate.)

HOSPITAL VISITATION

Upon Entering the Hospital

1

MEDITATION

Although you may be in a place of strange scenes, sounds, odors, and experiences, yet you are not among strange people. You are not alone. God is with you. These doctors and nurses here in the hospital are your friends. By their kindly ways and years of required training, they have been helping friends back to health and strength. For a few days this will be your home. Home is a place of love, friends, peace, and those who care.

A nurse is always on duty. If you ring for her, she will answer as soon as she is able. The doctors and attendants will respect your privacy, and you need feel no embarrassment. As your minister, I will come to see you from time to time. If you feel you need me at any time, please tell the nurse to call me. Most people who enter a hospital are soon well and strong again. With God's help you can face whatever the day may bring. Practice the presence of the Heavenly Father; it can take away all the strangeness and make this a place of confidence and trust.

SCRIPTURE

Cast all your anxieties on him, for he cares about you (1 Peter 5:7).

PASTOR'S PRAYER

Kind God, merciful Father: We pause in gratitude for this sanctuary of healing, and for every expression of love and unselfish concern. Grant that we may see behind those who wait upon us the presence of the Great Physician, who was compassionate, faithful, and kind. Use the wisdom of the doctors, the vigilant care of the nurses, the healing power of medicine, and the recreating influence of Thy Spirit; to hasten the recovery of this patient's health, we pray through Jesus Christ, the Lord. *Amen.*

2

MEDITATION

If all the facilities for "making people well" were seen at a glance, the sight would be astounding. If all the hospitals, equipment, laboratories, doctors, nurses, employees, money, and years of specialized training could be paraded before you, you would see what the world is doing for your recovery. The knowledge and experience of the past are at the doctor's disposal—for you.

The laws of nature are laws of healing. Bones knit. Wounds heal. Surgery gets rid of unwelcome "intruders" and lets nature do its normal work. All this is for you—and all others who are ill.[11]

SCRIPTURE

The Lord is near to all who call upon him (Psalms 145:18).

For God so loved the world that he gave his only Son, that whoever believes in him should not perish but have eternal life (John 3:16).

Bless the Lord, O my soul, and forget not all his benefits, who forgives all your iniquity, who heals all your diseases ... who crowns you with steadfast love and mercy, who satisfies you with good as long as you live (Psalms 103:2–5).

PASTOR'S PRAYER

Heavenly Father: How marvelous is the gift of life! In these quiet moments, we lift up our thoughts in gratitude for the dedication of men and women who have uncovered increasingly the mysteries of disease and have applied the best scientific insight to prolong the life span. We thank Thee for the progress made, and that this Thy child has had the good fortune of these benefits. Out of gratitude for these unmerited blessings, we would fill our days in useful service to Thee, through Jesus Christ. *Amen.*

Before an Operation

MEDITATION

As your body is being prepared for the coming surgery, allow God, your Creator, to prepare your mind. Relax and be at ease. As you trust your doctor and his assistants, so also trust the Great Physician. "Put your trust in the Lord." Have confidence in Him. "Bless the Lord, O my soul ... who healeth all thy diseases."

Let the "peace of God which passeth all understanding" be in your heart and mind. Let God do His work. "In quietness and confidence shall be your strength." You are God's child. He wants to help you in every way that you are capable of receiving His help. "Commit thy ways unto the Lord." Let Him speak peace to your heart.[12]

SCRIPTURE

Fear not, for I am with you (Isaiah 43:5).

PASTOR'S PRAYER

Our Father, who art never far away: We face this experience in trust, believing that Thy power and love are sufficient for our needs. Strengthen Thou this patient with inner peace. As the surgeon's hands are cleansed, so wash away any sins lurking in our subconscious minds. Bless the surgeon with skill to match the need. We commend to Thy safekeeping our life, both now and evermore. *Amen.*

Birth of a Baby

MEDITATION

In First Samuel, we read the account of Samuel's birth. Hannah and her husband, Elkanah, had no children. You know the pain and disappointment of having no children when your arms ache to hold one you can call your own. Hannah and Elkanah prayed earnestly to God that she might give birth to a son, vowing that if the prayer were answered the infant should be dedicated for life to Jehovah. The petition was granted, and they carried out their vow. They named the child Samuel, meaning "God-given."

In a very real sense this child is yours, and yet not yours. It belongs to you and yet does not belong to you. Parenthood is a God-given privilege; He originated life. The wisdom of the Almighty has placed this life into your care to mold and make, develop and shape, to prepare for life on earth and in eternity. You will be responsible to God for how you rear your child. May you have the faith and wisdom to match this great opportunity.

SCRIPTURE

Mary, the mother of Jesus, expressed her gratitude in these words: "My soul magnifies the Lord, and my spirit rejoices in God my Savior . . . for he who is mighty has done great things for me, and holy is his name" (Luke 1:46, 47, 49).

PASTOR'S PRAYER

Though we do not understand the mystery of physical birth, our Heavenly Father, we confess we have experienced a bit of heaven in this one's arrival. We thank Thee for Thy providence that has brought these to share in Thy creation, for the wondrous design of body and soul, and for the privilege of parenthood. Grant the child a strong body, a sound mind, and a sensitive spirit. Impress upon these parents the responsibility to Thee for the child's welfare, and bless them with patience, character, and good judgment, that this one may bring honor to Thee in the name of Jesus. *Amen.*

One Convalescing

MEDITATION

During recuperation, time may hang heavily on your hands. These suggestions may help you:

See to how many people you can give encouragement or a sincere word of appreciation; look about you and count the evidences of God's handiwork; read your New Testament, note especially in Luke, Jesus' concern for those who had physical ailments; write notes of appreciation to those who have been concerned over your illness; express appreciation to the nurses for their work and care; make a list of things you resolve to do for others when you are well and they are ill; give more time to personal devotions, praying especially for others in the hospital.[13]

SCRIPTURE

Bless the Lord, O my soul: and all that is within me, bless his holy name. Bless the Lord, O my soul, and forget not all his benefits: ... who healeth all thy diseases; ... who crowneth thee with lovingkindness and tender mercies (Psalms 103:1–4 KJV).

PASTOR'S PRAYER

Eternal God, our unfailing Guide and Friend: in the lonely hours we have felt Thee near—so near as to share with us. In our anxiety, weariness, and pain, we have had Thy peace and care and love. Thanks be unto Thee that Thy grace and power did minister to us. Thou art indeed the Good Shepherd, the Great Physician. The lesser things have dropped from view; the grander, nobler things have compelled our attention. All life has taken on new meaning. And now as we wait on Thee, give us patience, and be Thou patient with us a little longer. Set Thy purpose before us in all clarity. Renew us in health, in strength, in faith, as with a trustful spirit we look unto Thee. May this period of waiting be an opportunity of dedication. May Thy blessings, Lord, rest upon our beloved ones, upon all who have been in attendance, upon all who share the hospitality of this Temple of Healing. Keep us this day, tomorrow, and evermore, within Thy gracious keeping. Thine is the Kingdom, and the Power, and the Glory. *Amen.*[14]

Extreme Illness

MEDITATION

(said to family if patient is not conscious)

The doctors are doing everything within their power to sustain the life of your loved one. Whatever the outcome be, we must be prepared to leave it in the hands of God. We have not given up hope of recovery, for where faith is alive, hope is alive. If the body is beyond repair, however, we must be prepared for God to take the soul, and believe that "though the outward man is wasting away, the inward man is being renewed."

SCRIPTURE

The Lord is my light and my salvation; whom shall I fear? The Lord is the stronghold of my life; of whom shall I be afraid? (Psalms 27:1).

PASTORAL PRAYER

O God, who art a refuge of the distressed and the helper of the needy; out of the depths of our helplessness we turn to Thee. Grant us a sense of Thy presence, O Lord, that we will find comfort, assured that whatever may come, we are never beyond Thy love and care.

As this dear one has been brought near to death, help us to know that underneath are Thine everlasting arms. Our Father God, if this loved one can be brought back to health and life, it will fill our hearts with joy and thanksgiving. If, however, he must pass into the unseen future, we pray our friend may be raised out of the night of death into the light of that "inheritance, incorruptible and undefiled, and that fadeth not away," through Jesus Christ, our Lord. *Amen.*

PRAYERS FOR THE SICK

FOR ONE CRITICALLY ILL

O God—it is difficult to keep on hoping, when there seem to be constant setbacks and little progress.

I know quite well the doctors and nurses are very anxious about me. I've got to be ready for anything; it's pretty much touch and go. O God, give me the will to live and to fight this battle. Help me to have hope. After all, even on the darkest night, no one ever doubts that the morning will come again, and in the midst of winter, that spring is never far behind.

Help me to remember the skill You have given the physicians, and the recuperative powers You have given the body, and that with You, nothing is impossible.

If I am not able to get better, my Father, grant me the ability to accept it as a part of life, and to know that whether I live or die, nothing can separate me from Your love. Into Thy hands I commit myself. *Amen.*

WHEN DEPRESSED

O God, I am so utterly depressed—
I can't sleep—
I can't stop thinking—
I can't stop being afraid.
I feel I'll never get well—
Or be able to do anything again.

Or to be my old self.
The world goes on, and here I am, confined, isolated,
        forgotten.
Lord, I can't cope with it any longer!
I am beaten unless you help me—
        No one else seems to be able to help.
So God—please—please!
Stop my thoughts going 'round and 'round—
        Stop my worry and help me forget—
        Stop my tense nervousness.
Put Your hand in my hand—
        put Your hope into my hopelessness—
        put Your strength into my weakness—
        put Your peace in my mind—
        put a new song in my mouth—
        put a new Spirit in my heart.

I cast my burden upon You—believing You will sustain me.
Amen.

EYES TO SEE BEAUTY

Lover and Source of all beauty, You have made all things
beautiful to behold. Grant me eyes to see—
The glory of daybreak with the returning of light . . .
the refreshment from a cup of cold water on dry parched
    lips . . .
the dedication and compassion underlying nurses' care,
    and the minister's visits . . .
the blending of colors I have never taken time to view . . .
the blessing of quietness and the fascination of strange
    sounds, the meaning in understanding words, and the
    mystery of communications.
Save me, Lord, from seeing only the ugly, dismal, difficult
side of everything, by seeing through the eyes of Jesus. *Amen.*

IN SILENT TIMES

O God, who art known by those who can be quiet, who
speaks in the silent vigils of life, grant me to "be still and know
Thou art God"!
Divert my mind from the noisy, discordant sounds of the

world, that I might be aware of Thy blessings that come in silence.

Silently, the new green leaves grow to full size. Silently, flowers come to bloom and as silently fade away.

Silently, the earth moves around the sun; silently it turns on its axis, bringing day and night; silently it tilts, so changing the seasons.

Silently, a baby grows to adulthood. Silently the sick are made well with healing.

As Phillips Brooks wrote,

> How silently, how silently
>   The Wondrous gift is given!
> So God imparts to human hearts
>   The blessings of His heaven.

O Divine Spirit, in my quiet time now, come, with Thy heavenly blessings. *Amen.*

AT EVENING

As darkness descends upon the earth, creeping through the valleys, quietly putting the day to sleep, grant that the Holy Spirit of peace may fall upon my being. To Thee, from whom I have received the gift of today, I return the parcel filled to completion, wrapped in my thoughts, tied with tender memories and sealed in gratitude.

Eternal Light, shine within me even in the darkness, that I may have light—not of the sun but of the soul—not for the eye but for the mind.

Grant me light by which to judge my errors and to see Thy path through the tangled ways of the world.

Bring to me now, O Lord, the healing touch of sleep, and the calmness of trustful rest in Thee, Holy Spirit of Peace. *Amen.*

THE POWER TO TRIUMPH

God of my destiny—

I am not asking for any special favors as though I were a special child and You were a Celestial Protector. I am not asking for escape from the liabilities of being human. I don't want anything heroic; I don't want to bargain with You.

God—I just want to be able to bear the things I have to face. I am asking for inward resources to face suffering and pain without grumbling or complaining, without whining or self-pity. I want You to be proud of my courage and maturity. Through this experience, may I grow in character and patience, in compassion and love, in self-control and prayer.

Lord Jesus, I am glad You went through all You did, because it means You understand exactly how I feel. Help me to triumph as You did. *Amen.*

THANKSGIVING FOR HEALING

Gracious Companion of my Spirit, I thank You for the recovery I am making. It is good to be able to taste and like food again, to get my feet on the floor again and walk; to be able to do a few things for myself; to visit with friends; to read books and watch television.

I am so grateful just to have the joy of feeling myself again! Keep me humbly mindful of all the people who helped me back to health—the doctors, the nurses, the minister, the loved ones, the friends, and above all, to You, O God, without whom no healing is possible.

Now that I will soon be going home, give me the discipline not to do too much too soon. Help me to be obedient to those who know what is best for me. Continue to give me patience, for in the end all things will pass, and there will be no more pain. *Amen.*

APPROPRIATE SCRIPTURE READINGS

1

CONFIDENCE IN GOD

The Lord is my shepherd, I shall not want; he makes me lie down in green pastures. He leads me beside still waters; he restores my soul. He leads me in paths of righteousness for his name's sake. Even though I walk through the valley of the shadow of death, I fear no evil; for thou art with me; thy rod and thy staff, they comfort me. Thou preparest a table before me in the presence of my enemies; thou anointest my head with oil, my cup overflows. Surely goodness and mercy shall follow me all the days of my life; and I shall dwell in the house of the Lord for ever (Psalm 23).

2

GOD AS MY FORTRESS

He who dwells in the shelter of the Most High, who abides in the shadow of the Almighty, will say to the Lord, "My refuge and my fortress; my God in whom I trust." For he will deliver you from the snare of the fowler and from the deadly pestilence; he will cover you with his pinions, and under his wings you will find refuge; his faithfulness is a shield and buckler (Psalms 91:1–4).

3

THE ETERNITY OF GOD

Lord, thou hast been our dwelling place in all generations. Before the mountains were brought forth, or ever thou hadst formed the earth and the world, from everlasting to everlasting thou art God (Psalms 90:1, 2).

4

MY STRENGTH COMETH FROM GOD

I lift up my eyes to the hills. From whence does my help come? My help comes from the Lord, who made heaven and earth. He will not let your foot be moved, he who keeps you will not slumber. Behold, he who keeps Israel will neither slumber nor sleep. The Lord is your keeper; the Lord is your shade on your right hand. The sun shall not smite you by day, nor the moon by night. The Lord will keep you from all evil; he will keep your life. The Lord will keep your going out and your coming in from this time forth and for evermore (Psalm 121).

5

RELEASE FROM WORRY

Therefore I tell you, do not be anxious about your life, what you shall eat or what you shall drink, nor about your body, what you shall put on. Is not life more than food, and the body more than clothing? Look at the birds of the air: they neither sow nor reap nor gather into barns, and yet your heavenly Father feeds them. Are you not of more value than they? And which of you by being anxious can add one cubit to his span of life? (Matthew 6:25–27).

6

FORGET TODAY'S CONCERN

And why are you anxious about clothing? Consider the lilies of the field, how they grow; they neither toil nor spin; yet I tell you, even Solomon in all his glory was not arrayed like one of these. But if God so clothes the grass of the field, which today is alive and tomorrow is thrown into the oven, will he not much more clothe you, O men of little faith? Therefore do not be anxious, saying, "What shall we eat?" or "What shall we drink?" or "What shall we wear?" For the Gentiles seek all these things; and your heavenly Father knows that you need them all. But seek first his kingdom and his righteousness, and all these things shall be yours as well. Therefore do not be anxious about tomorrow, for tomorrow will be anxious for itself. Let the day's own trouble be sufficient for the day (Matthew 6:28–34).

7

ASK AND RECEIVE

Ask, and it will be given to you; seek and you will find; knock, and it will be opened to you. For every one who asks receives, and he who seeks finds, and to him who knocks it will be opened (Matthew 7:7, 8).

8

UNTO THE WEARY AND CONTRITE

Come to me, all who labor and are heavy-laden, and I will give you rest. Take my yoke upon you, and learn from me; for I am gentle and lowly in heart, and you will find rest for your souls. For my yoke is easy, and my burden is light (Matthew 11:28–30).

9

ON FAITH

Then the disciples came to Jesus privately and said, "Why could we not cast it out?" He said to them, "Because of your little faith. For truly, I say to you, if you have faith as a grain of mustard seed, you will say to this mountain, 'Move hence to yonder place,' and it will move; and nothing will be impossible to you" (Matthew 17:19, 20).

10

WHEN ANXIOUS

Don't worry about anything, but in all your prayers ask God for what you need, always asking him with a thankful heart. And God's peace, which is far beyond human understanding, will keep your hearts and minds safe in union with Christ Jesus (Philippians 4:6, 7 TEV).

I look to the Lord for help at all times, and he rescues me from danger. Turn to me, Lord, and be merciful to me, because I am lonely and weak. Relieve me of my worries and save me from all my troubles. Consider my distress and suffering and forgive all my sins (Psalms 25:15–18 TEV).

We know that in all things God works for good with those who love him, those whom he has called according to his purpose. Those whom God had already chosen he also set apart to become like his Son, so that the Son would be the first among many brothers. And so those whom God set apart, he called; and those he called, he put right with himself, and he shared his glory with them (Romans 8:28–30 TEV).

11

GOD PROMISES STRENGTH

Israel, why then do you complain that the Lord doesn't know your troubles or care if you suffer injustice? Don't you know? Haven't you heard? The Lord is the everlasting God; he created all the world. He never grows tired or weary. No one understands his thoughts. He strengthens those who are weak and tired. Even those who are young grow weak; young men can fall exhausted. But those who trust in the Lord for help will find their strength renewed. They will rise on wings like eagles; they will run and not get weary; they will walk and not grow weak (Isaiah 40:27–31 TEV).

12

GOD PROMISES FAITHFULNESS

O Lord, I will always sing of your constant love; I will proclaim your faithfulness forever. I know that your love will last for all time, that your faithfulness is as permanent as the sky. You said, "I have made a convenant with the man I chose; I have promised my servant David, a descendant of yours will always be king; I will preserve your dynasty forever."

The heavens sing of the wonderful things you do; the holy ones sing of your faithfulness, Lord. No one in heaven is like you, Lord; none of the heavenly beings is your equal. You are feared in the council of the holy ones; they all stand in awe of you. Lord God Almighty, none is as mighty as you; in all things you are faithful, O Lord (Psalms 89:1–8 TEV).

Remember Jesus Christ, who was raised from death, who was a descendant of David, as is taught in the Good News I preach. Because I preach the Good News, I suffer and I am even chained like a criminal. But the Word of God is not in chains, and so I endure everything for the sake of God's chosen people, in order that they too may obtain the salvation that comes through Christ Jesus and brings eternal glory. This is a true saying:

> If we have died with him,
>   we shall also live with him.
> If we continue to endure,
>   we shall also rule with him.
> If we deny him,
>   he also will deny us.
> If we are not faithful,
>   he remains faithful,
>   because he cannot be false
>   to himself.
>
> 2 Timothy 2:8–13 TEV

The thought of my pain, my homelessness, is bitter poison. I think of it constantly, and my spirit is depressed. Yet my hope returns when I remember this one thing: The Lord's unfailing love and mercy still continue, fresh as the morning, as sure as the sunrise. The Lord is all I have, and so in him I put my hope (Lamentations 3:19–24 TEV).

13

HIS PEACE

May you always be joyful in your union with the Lord. I say it again: rejoice!

Show a gentle attitude toward everyone. The Lord is coming soon. Don't worry about anything, but in all your prayers ask God for what you need, always asking him with a thankful heart. And God's peace, which is far beyond human understanding, will keep your hearts and minds safe in union with Christ Jesus.

In conclusion, my brothers, fill your minds with those things that are good and that deserve praise: things that are true, noble, right, pure, lovely, and honorable. Put into practice what you learned and received from me, both from my words and from my actions. And God who gives us peace will be with you (Philippians 4:4–9 TEV).

I am listening to what the Lord God is saying; he promises peace to us, his own people, if we do not go back to our foolish ways. Surely he is ready to save those who honor him, and his saving presence will remain in our land.

Love and faithfulness will meet; righteousness and peace will embrace. Man's loyalty will reach up from the earth, and God's righteousness will look down from heaven. The Lord will make us prosperous, and our land will produce rich harvests. Righteousness will go before the Lord and prepare the path for him (Psalms 85:8–13 TEV).

14

HIS FORGIVENESS

Praise the Lord, my soul! All my being, praise his holy name! Praise the Lord, my soul, and do not forget how kind he is. He forgives all my sins and heals all my diseases. He keeps me from the grave and blesses me with love and mercy. He fills my life with good things, so that I stay young and strong like an eagle.

The Lord judges in favor of the oppressed and gives them their rights. He revealed his plans to Moses and let the people of Israel see his mighty deeds. The Lord is merciful and loving, slow to become angry and full of constant love. He does not keep on rebuking; he is not angry forever. He does not punish us as we deserve or repay us according to our sins and wrongs. As high as the sky is above the earth, so great is his love for those who have reverence for him. As far as the east is from the west, so far does he remove our sins from us. As a father is kind to his children, so the Lord is kind to those who honor him. He knows what we are made of; he remembers that we are dust (Psalms 103:1–14 TEV).

Let us give thanks to the God and Father of our Lord Jesus Christ! For in our union with Christ he has blessed us by giving us every spiritual blessing in the heavenly world. Even before the world was made, God had already chosen us to be his through our union with Christ, so that we would be holy and without fault before him.

Because of his love God had already decided that through Jesus Christ he would make us his sons—this was his pleasure and purpose. Let us praise God for his glorious grace, for the free gift he gave us in his dear Son! For by the sacrificial death of Christ we are set free, that is, our sins are forgiven. How great is the grace of God, which he gave to us in such large measure! (Ephesians 1:3–8 TEV).

15

HIS LOVE

In view of all this, what can we say? If God is for us, who can be against us? Certainly not God, who did not even keep back his own Son, but offered him for us all! He gave us his Son— will he not also freely give us all things? Who will accuse God's chosen people? God himself declares them not guilty! Who, then, will condemn them? Not Christ Jesus, who died, or rather, who was raised to life and is at the right side of God, pleading with him for us! Who, then, can separate us from the love of Christ? Can trouble do it, or hardship or persecution or hunger or poverty or danger or death? As the scripture says, "For your sake we are in danger of death at all times; we are treated like sheep that are going to be slaughtered." No, in all these things we have complete victory through him who loved us. For I am certain that nothing can separate us from his love: neither death nor life, neither angels nor other heavenly rulers or powers, neither the present nor the future, neither the world above nor the world below—there is nothing in all creation that will ever be able to separate us from the love of God which is ours through Christ Jesus our Lord (Romans 8:31–39 TEV).

HOMEBOUND COMMUNION

(*The communion emblems are taken by the church elders or minister to the recipient.*)

Call to Worship   Man does not live on bread alone but on every word that comes from the mouth of God.

Invocation Prayer   O Lord, we come here as on sacred ground, to handle these sacred emblems, with this, our friend. Blest be the tie that binds our hearts in Christian love, in Jesus' name.

Scripture

> O Lord, thou hast searched me and known me!
> Thou knowest when I sit down and when I rise up;
>   thou discernest my thoughts from afar.
> Thou searchest out my path and my lying down,
>   and art acquainted with all my ways,
> Even before a word is on my tongue,
>   lo, O Lord, thou knowest it altogether.
>
> For thou didst form my inward parts,
>   thou didst knit me together in my mother's womb.
>
> Search me, O God, and know my heart!
>   Try me and know my thoughts!
> And see if there be any wicked way in me,
>   and lead me in the way everlasting!
>   Psalms 13:1–4, 13, 23–24

Prayer of Confession

Lord God, we thank You for Jesus Christ, by whose life, death, and Resurrection, all creation is being reconciled and perfected. In Him our lives are overcoming weakness and fading strength; overcoming sin and finding grace; overcoming imperfection and becoming more complete. O Lord, make our souls receptive to this bread and this drink, so that we may experience your Holy Spirit working within us to fulfill Your divine image, in Jesus' name. *Amen.*

Words of Pardon   Isn't it comforting to know the promise is true, "that everyone who believes in him [Jesus] will have their sins forgiven through his name?" (Acts 10:43 TLB). Thanks be to God!

Invitation   All of your friends of the church join me in sharing these emblems of Jesus, our Lord and Friend, with you.

Words of Institution   1 Corinthians 11:23–25 TLB

FOR THE BREAD   "This is what the Lord himself has said about his Table, and I passed it on to you before: That on the night when Judas betrayed him, the Lord Jesus took bread, and when he had given thanks to God for it, he broke it and gave it to his disciples and said, "Take this and eat it. This is my body which is given for you. Do this to remember me.' "

FOR THE CUP   "In the same way, he took the cup of wine after supper, saying, 'This cup is the new agreement between God and you that has been established and set in motion by my blood. Do this in remembrance of me. . . .' "

Words of Assurance   Jesus said, "Anyone eating this bread shall live forever" (John 6:51 TLB).

Passing of the Peace (*double handclasp*)   May the peace of God be with your spirit.

NURSING HOME SERVICE

Give to each person coming to the worship service a button to wear with a SMILE—GOD LOVES YOU *slogan. Take a banner or two for the gathering area with slogans such as,* LOVE LIFE, CELE-BRATE; CHOOSE LIFE; GOD IS LOVE; GOD LOVES YOU . . . SMILE!

A song service is conducted with guitars, using all kinds of gospel hymns, popular radio religious songs, with special-request time.

There should also be a time for Scripture recitation of favorite biblical passages.

Prayers of Intercession for persons and concerns mentioned. (Procedures possible: Each person's name is put on a piece of paper, placed in a box. Then each person draws out a name for whom he or she prays; or, concerns may be called out orally and the LEADER *prays; or, sentence prayers may be given by those who wish from among the worshipers.*)

Meditation   (*brief, not more than six minutes*)

THE TOUCH OF LOVE

Do you believe God loves you? Do you? Do you feel God's love permeating your being?

The way to get past the far-away, stern, warlike God of the Old Testament is to begin with Christ. This button I am wearing says, SMILE—GOD LOVES YOU. Love Christ and enjoy God. It's as simple as that!

Christ came to show us a tender, loving, concerned, and forgiving God. Christ knew how to love people and this love is the essence of God.

Have you ever felt abused, neglected, unwanted, extra baggage? Have you been filled with resentment and bitterness? You need to love and to be loved in return.

When a child is ill, injured, or scared by a thunderstorm or a bad dream, he seeks a parent. He wants to be held, touched, or snuggled up. Human contact!

Jesus always touched the persons He healed. There is an outflowing from one person to another in the human touch. A woman, afflicted by bleeding, reached out just to touch the robe Jesus was wearing. In the contact, she was healed.

Try an experiment. Turn to the person nearest you. Put your hands together, as though for prayer. Let your neighbor put his or her hands over yours. Then let the person with hands on the outside say, "God bless you!"

Did you feel it? It's more powerful than words. It's the touch of love. Touch is important.

When God decided to give us Christmas to commemorate His love for us, He did it with touch. He sent His Son, in human form, to touch us. That's why in everything important in the church—baptism, receiving new members, ordination, healing—the touch is important. Love is communicated in touch!

An Alternate Meditation

"LENGTH OF DAYS"

"Length of days," was thought to be a peculiar and cherished blessing promised to Abraham, David, Job, and untold millions. Who among us does not agree? Why else do we strive to prolong life?

Long life multiplies the opportunities for service in glorifying God. When a person's life is prematurely cut short, what a shame! I am thinking of Raphael, the artist, who died in his thirties; of Jesus Christ, who was murdered at the age of thirty-three; of thousands of military boys, whose lives have been snuffed out in young adulthood; of children, whose potentials never had a chance to blossom. What tragedy! How unfortunate! What loss to the world! What a privilege to live to full age. Think of the mature judgment, usefulness, and labor of many years. Think of the accomplishments of those in sunset years.

Titian painted his masterpiece *The Battle of Lepanto* at the age of ninety-eight; Verdi wrote his great opera *Otello* at seventy-four, and *Falstaff* at eighty. Kant, at seventy-four, wrote his anthropology; Edison built chemical plants after he was sixty-seven; General MacArthur was Supreme Commander of the occupation in Japan in his seventies. Socrates learned to play a musical instrument in his old age; Canto, at eighty, studied Greek; Plutarch, almost as old, studied Latin. Dr. Samuel Johnson applied himself to the Dutch language only a few years before his death; yet one morning in later life, he amused himself by committing to memory eight hundred lines of *Virgil;* at the age of seventy-three, while suffering from an attack of paralysis so severe that it rendered him speechless, he composed a Latin prayer in order to test the condition of his mental facilities. Chaucer's *Canterbury Tales* were the composition of his later years. They were begun in his forty-seventh year and finished in his sixty-first. Franklin's *Philosophical Pursuits* began when he had nearly reached his fiftieth year. Sir Christopher Wren retired from public life at eighty-six; after that he spent five years in literary, astronomical, and religious pursuits. Necker offers a beautiful instance of the influence of late studies in life when he tells us, "The era of three scores and ten is an agreeable age for writing; your mind has not lost its vigor, and envy leaves you in peace."

(*Following the Meditation, have a moment when each person touches the other persons near him with the words* "God loves you, and I love you.")

Benediction

The Lord bless you and keep you: The Lord make his face to shine upon you, and be gracious to you: The Lord lift up his countenance upon you, and give you peace. *Amen* (Numbers 6:24–26).

COMMUNION TO THE SICK

Opening Sentence   God so loved the world that he gave his only Son, that whoever believes in him should not perish but have eternal life (John 3:16).

Invocation   Almighty God, unto whom all hearts are open, all desires known, and from whom no secrets are hid; Cleanse the thoughts of our hearts by the inspiration of Thy Holy Spirit, that we may perfectly love Thee and worthily magnify Thy holy name. Through Christ our Lord. *Amen.*

Scripture Reading   The Lord is my shepherd, I shall not want; he makes me lie down in green pastures. He leads me beside still waters; he restores my soul. He leads me in paths of righteousness for his name's sake. Even though I walk through the valley of the shadow of death, I fear no evil; for thou art with me; thy rod and thy staff, they comfort me. Thou preparest a table before me in the presence of my enemies; thou anointest my head with oil, my cup overflows. Surely goodness and mercy shall follow me all the days of my life; and I shall dwell in the house of the Lord for ever (Psalm 23).

Communion Meditation   The cup of blessing which we bless, is it not a participation in the blood of Christ? The bread which we break, is it not a participation in the body of Christ? (1 Corinthians 10:16).

In the broken bread, Christ offered to share with us His life. The Christian who comes to the Lord's table receives a share in the sinless and holy life of Christ which helps to redeem the lives of all. This bread of the communion service is a means of participation in Christ's Body, the Church.

Likewise, in the cup Christ offered us a share in His atoning death. When we drink of the cup, we declare our readiness to share His sufferings, to shed our blood, and to claim the victory of the eventual departure from this life.

To participate in the death and in the life of Christ is to be identified with the triumph of His Resurrection. He gave us fellowship at the most ultimate levels of existence—life and death. Every person has one of each. The emblems symbolize the redemption of life and the redemption of death. As we partake, we are identified with Christ in both.

Prayer of Thanks for the Bread and Cup   Dear Lord and Father of us all: We thank Thee for this bread and cup which remind us of Thy great love for us as expressed in the life, death, and Resurrection of Jesus Christ our Saviour. We draw near to Thee in humility and reverence, confessing our sins, knowing that in Thee we will find forgiveness, refuge, hope, and salvation, now and forever. *Amen.*

Words of Institution for the Bread   And as they were eating, he took bread, and blessed, and broke it, and gave it to them, and said, "Take; this is my body" (Mark 14:22).

Words of Institution for the Cup   And he took a cup, and when he had given thanks he gave it to them, and they all drank of it. And he said to them, "This is my blood of the covenant, which is poured out for many" (Mark 14:23, 24).

Lord's Prayer in Unison

Benediction   The Lord bless you and keep you: The Lord make his face to shine upon you, and be gracious to you: The Lord lift up his countenance upon you, and give you peace (Numbers 6:24–26).

Section 4

THE WEDDING SERVICE

Marriage—Under God's Law

Traditional Wedding Ceremony

Home Wedding

Contemporary Sanctuary Wedding

Blessing of a Civil Marriage

MARRIAGE—UNDER GOD'S LAW

Ceremonies are important in life to make public what we feel in our hearts, to openly declare our commitments, to celebrate significant occasions with families and friends. The wedding ceremony is perhaps the most meaningful ritual of all.

It is God's law, even more than the state's, that gives two people the right to live together. Therefore, a religious ceremony is the most appropriate; a church is the most consistent place to celebrate Christian marriage; and a minister, as God's representative, is the most proper presider.

Persons planning weddings are inclined to overemphasize the reception, floral decorations, impressive apparel, glamour, prewedding parties, and photographs, with little attention to the counseling preparation, the content of the ceremony, and the significance of marriage in the Church.

Recognizing the diversity of views and practices, the following material is presented.

TRADITIONAL WEDDING CEREMONY

(*Prepared by Dr. G. Edwin Osborne*)

At the day and time appointed for solemnization of matrimony, the persons to be married shall come into the body of the church, or shall be ready in some proper house, with their friends and neighbors; and there, standing together, the man on the right hand, and the woman on the left, the minister shall say:

May God be gracious to us and bless us, and make His face to shine upon us, through Jesus Christ our Lord. *Amen.*

When Jesus was invited with His disciples to the marriage,

He gladly accepted the invitation, and there began His ministry and His acts of power. Thus also we are now assembled, to be after Him witnesses of the pledges this man and this woman are to make to each other, and to set them forth in their new estate of marriage by our prayers and Christian greetings.

Let us pray: Our eternal Father, whose very nature is love, and from whom cometh every good and perfect gift; look with Thy favor upon these Thy servants who desire to make their vows before Thee, and to seek Thy blessing upon the solemn engagement to which they now pledge themselves.

Send down upon them, we beseech Thee, Thy heavenly benediction; bestow upon them the gift of Thy Holy Spirit, that He may sanctify their love and be Himself the unity between them; keep them ever faithful to their holy covenant, and may they live together all their days in true love and perfect peace; through Jesus Christ our Lord. *Amen.*

Then shall the minister say:

Who gives this woman to be married to this man?

Then the father, or whoever takes his place, shall answer:

I do.

Then, speaking to the persons who are to be married, the minister shall say:

The rite of marriage in which you two come now to be united is the first and oldest rite of the world, celebrated since the beginning of the human race. Long before men had developed ceremony or inaugurated priests, marriage was celebrated, with God the creator its first priest and witness and guest. It is His institution for the comfort and convenience of mankind, and is therefore enshrined with dignity and honor for all who enter into it lawfully and in true affection.

Marriage was confirmed by Christ's solemn Word, and adorned and blessed by His presence at the wedding feast in Cana of Galilee. It is set forth in the New Testament as signifying the mystical union between Christ and His Church. It is a sacrament of grace to all who enter into it under the blessing of God, and it will remain to them a bond of happiness and peace so long as His presence is kept in their hearts to sanctify the love between them.

Thus marriage will be to you, if you have it in your hearts to beautify and enrich it by your tender devotions, your mindfulness in little things, your patience and sacrifice of self to each other. All of which I charge on you here in God's sight to remember and to do, even as you will ever pray for yourselves.

To signify your willingness to engage upon these obligations, and as a seal of the holy vows you are now to make, you will join your right hands.

Then shall the minister say to the man:

Will you, _____, take _____, whom you hold by the hand, to be your wedded wife; promising to keep, cherish, and defend her, and to be her faithful and true husband so long as you both shall live?

The man shall answer:

I will.

Then shall the minister say to the woman:

Will you, _____, take _____, whom you hold by the hand, to be your wedded husband; promising to adhere unchangeably to him in all life's changes, and to be his loving and true wife so long as you both shall live?

The woman shall answer:

I will.

Single-Ring Service

. . . Then shall they loose their hands, and the minister shall say to the man:

_____, will you seal your sacred troth by the giving of a ring in pledge that you will faithfully perform your vows?

The man shall answer:

I will.

The man, receiving the ring from his groomsman, delivers it to the minister, who says:

This ring is of precious metal; so let your love be the most precious possession of your hearts. It is a circle, unbroken; so let your love each for the other be unbroken through all your earthly days.

Then shall the minister say to the woman:

_____, as a token and a pledge that you will faithfully perform your holy vows, will you so receive and wear this ring?

The woman shall answer:

I will.

Then the minister, addressing the man, shall say:

Forasmuch as the husband imparts to his wife his name, and receives her into his care and keeping, I give you this ring that you may place it on the finger of your bride as a token, and in pledge that you so receive her.

Thus you are to compass about her life with strength and protecting love.

Addressing the woman, the minister continues:

Thus you are to wear this ring as the enclosing bond of reverence and trust.

Addressing both the man and the woman, the minister continues:

Thus you both are to fulfill the perfect circle of duty that makes you one.

Double-Ring Service

Then shall they loose their hands, and the minister shall say to them:

Will you each seal your sacred troth by the giving of a ring in pledge that you will faithfully perform your vows?

The man and woman each shall answer:

I will.

The man, receiving the ring from his groomsman, and the woman, from the maid of honor, deliver them to the minister, who says:

These rings are of precious metal; so let your love be the most precious possession of your hearts. Each is a circle unbroken; so let your love, one for the other, be unbroken through all your earthly days.

Then shall the minister say to the woman:

_____, as a token and a pledge that you will faith-
fully perform your holy vows, will you so receive and wear this
ring?

The woman shall answer:

I will.

Then the minister, addressing the man, shall say:

_____, indicating your responsibility to
_____ to receive her into your care and keeping, I
give you this ring that you may place it on her finger as a
token, and in pledge that you so receive her. Thus you are to
compass about her life with strength and protecting love.

Then shall the minister say to the man:

_____, as a token and a pledge that you will faith-
fully perform your holy vows, will you receive and wear this
ring?

The man shall answer:

I will.

Then the minister, addressing the woman, shall say:

_____, indicating your responsibility to
_____ to receive him into your care and devotion, I
give you this ring that you may place it on his finger as a token
and in pledge that you so receive him. Thus you are to encircle
his life with affection and tenderness.

*Addressing both the man and the woman, the minister con-
tinues:*

Thus you each are to wear your ring as the enclosing bond of
reverence and trust.

Thus you both are to fulfill the perfect circle of duty that
makes you one.

*Following the ceremony of the ring (or rings), then the minister
shall say:*

And now I charge that you love one another, as ordained of
God:

Love is patient and kind; love is not jealous or boastful; it is
not arrogant or rude. Love does not insist on its own way; it is

not irritable or resentful; it does not rejoice at wrong, but rejoices in the right. Love bears all things, believes all things,
hopes all things, endures all things. Love never ends.... So
faith, hope, love abide, these three; but the greatest of these is
love (1 Corinthians 13:4–8, 13).

Let us pray.

*Then the man and the woman kneeling, the minister, and the
people shall say the Lord's Prayer:*

Our Father, who art in heaven, hallowed be Thy name. Thy
kingdom come, Thy will be done on earth as it is in heaven.
Give us this day our daily bread; and forgive us our debts, as
we forgive our debtors; and lead us not into temptation, but deliver us from evil; for thine is the kingdom and the power and
the glory forever. *Amen.*

Then shall the minister add:

Most merciful and gracious Father, of whom the whole family in heaven and earth is named; bestow upon these Thy servants the seal of thine approval and Thy fatherly benediction;
granting them to fulfill, with pure and steadfast affection, the
vow and covenant between them made. Guide them together,
we pray, in the way of righteousness and peace, that loving and
serving Thee, with one heart and mind, all the days of their
lives, they may be abundantly enriched with the tokens of
thine everlasting favor; in Jesus Christ our Lord. *Amen.*

Then shall the minister join their right hands together, and say:

Those whom God has joined together let no man put asun-
der.

Then shall the minister, addressing the man and woman, say:

For as much as you, _____, and you,
_____, have convenanted together in the presence of
God, and of this company, to live together in holy marriage,
and have pledged the same by giving and receiving a ring, and
by joining hands; I declare you to be husband and wife, in the
name of the Father, and of the Son, and of the Holy Spirit.

Then the minister shall add this blessing:

The Lord bless you and keep you. The Lord make His face

to shine upon you, and be gracious to you. The Lord lift up His countenance upon you and give you peace. *Amen.*

The minister may add this benediction:

And now may He who walked in intimate companionship with the first human pair in the days of their innocence; and He who coming in sorrow made the marriage feast to rejoice by his miraculous ministry; and He who dwelling in your hearts can make your house a habitation of love and peace— the Father, Son, and Holy Spirit—be with you evermore. *Amen.*

HOME WEDDING

Gathering music may be a medley of contemporary love songs played by guitars or, if necessary, recordings. An altar area with prie-dieu, flowers, and candelabra is arranged in the largest room. Flute music is light and joyful for the processional.

MINISTER   Married love has been, from the beginning of time, enshrined in dignity and honor. It is the bond wherein is realized the divine in human life.

It is not to be entered into flippantly nor temporarily, but only with integrity, personal commitment, and in godly reverence and love.

Into this holy relationship, these two persons come now to be joined.

Let us pray: Eternal Father, whose very nature is love, look with favor upon these people who desire to make their vows of commitment, and who seek Your blessings and those of their families and friends, in the love of Jesus Christ our Lord. *Amen.*

We were made to love and to be loved. We walk this earth as unfinished creations until we find fulfillment in the love of others. Those of us who were fortunate found the greatest significance in our childhood lives when we were able to share our joys and fears, our triumphs and sorrows, in the love of parents and brothers and sisters. As our growing lives extended beyond the home, we found meaning and enrichment in the love of a few sincere friends. Emerging into maturity, the hunger of the lonely soul brings us to the greatest thing in human life, the love between man and woman. Here, we have the fusion of two personalities—a new creation—and human incompleteness has found divine fulfillment. As each of you sacrifices some freedom to the covenant between you, you will find greater freedom from loneliness and self-concern. As each of you pledges exclusive devotion to the other, you will find a flood of tenderness welling up within you which can become a passion for the welfare of all mankind. As each of you shares the innermost experiences with the other, you will find that God is dwelling in your midst. I am very happy for you, _____ and _____, for you have found the key that can unlock the universe to the hearts of men.

MINISTER   (*to* GROOM) _____, will you have _____ to be your wedded wife, to live together after God's ordinance in the holy estate of matrimony?

GROOM   I will.

MINISTER   (*to* BRIDE) _____, will you have _____ to be your wedded husband, to live together after God's ordinance in the holy estate of matrimony?

BRIDE   I will.

MINISTER   Who presents this bride in marriage?

FATHER OF BRIDE   Her mother and I do.

1 Corinthians, 13:4–7 (TEV)   Love is patient and kind; love is not jealous, or conceited, or proud; love is not ill-mannered, or selfish, or irritable; love does not keep a record of wrongs; love is not happy with evil, but is happy with the truth. Love never gives up; its faith, hope, and patience never fail.

GROOM   I, _____, accept you, _____, as my wedded wife to share in the fullness of Christian living as long as we both shall live.

BRIDE   I, _____, accept you, _____, as my wedded husband to share in the fullness of Christian living as long as we both shall live.

MINISTER   What symbol do you now exchange as an outward sign of your love?

Let us pray: O God, may these rings ever signify the love of these two. As these circles are fashioned without an ending, they speak of eternity. May the incorruptible substance of these rings represent a love glowing with increasing luster through the years. *Amen.*

GROOM   With this wedding ring, I pledge my love and loyalty forever. Your people shall be my people.

BRIDE   With this wedding ring, I pledge my love and loyalty forever. Wherever you go, I will go, and wherever you dwell, I will dwell.

MINISTER   Let us pray: O God, as You love these two, so may they love each other. In their new responsibilities, grant them the gift of warmth in all their relationships, the gift of common sense in meeting their problems, and the gift of communication in deepening their union, through the Spirit of Jesus Christ. *Amen.*

Since _____ and _____ have exchanged your vows according to the laws of _____ and in the presence of this company, but more importantly in the presence of God, I, with the authority invested in me as a minister of the Gospel of Jesus Christ, announce you to be husband and wife.

Will you kneel for the benediction?

Benediction

MINISTER   May the Lord fill you with all spiritual benediction and grace that you may live together in the fullness of life.

May you have peace—
  Not of the stagnant pool, but of deep waters, flowing.
May you have poise—
  Not of the sheltered tree, but of the oak, deep-rooted, storm-strengthened, and free.
May you have power—
  Not of fisted might, but of the quickened seed stretching toward infinite light. In Jesus' name. *Amen.*

SOLO   "One Hand—One Heart"

Symbolic Candle Lighting   (BRIDE *and* GROOM *rise, take the outside lighted candles of a three-pronged candelabrum, and together light the center candle, then extinguish the two outside candles.*)

MINISTER   "... It is not good that man should be alone.... Therefore a man leaves his father and his mother, and cleaves to his wife, and they become one flesh" (Genesis 2:18, 24). As two lights are now blended into one, so two lives are blended into one.

May you be one in name, one in aim, and one in happy destiny together.

(GROOM *kisses the* BRIDE. *As couple turns, facing the congregation,* MINISTER *says:*)

I present Mr. and Mrs. _____. Congratulations are now in order.

The Kiss of Peace   (*Each person kisses the* BRIDE *and* GROOM *on the cheek and gives a personal blessing.*)

CONTEMPORARY SANCTUARY WEDDING

The Organ Recital

Rejoice Greatly, O My Soul .... Karg-Elert
Jesu, Joy of Man's Desiring .... Bach-Grace
Basse et Dessus de Trompette .... Cherambault
From God I Ne'er Will Turn Me ...... Buxtehude
Suite Gothique .... Boellmann
Sarabande .... Bach-Phillips
Rhosymedre ("Lovely") .... Williams
O Perfect Love .... Barnby

THE PROCESSIONAL HYMN   "Love Divine, All Love Excelling" (*the* CONGREGATION *standing and singing*)

Sentences of Worship

MINISTER   "It is not good that the man should be alone" (Genesis 2:18).

"Therefore a man leaves his father and his mother, and cleaves to his wife; and they become one flesh" (Genesis 2:24).

The quality of love for all of life's relationships has been described by the Apostle Paul in his unforgettable words from his First Letter to the Corinthians, Chapter 13: "I may speak in tongues of men or of angels, but if I am without love, I am a sounding gong or a clanging cymbal. I may have the gift of prophecy, and know every hidden truth; I may have faith strong enough to move mountains; but if I have no love, I am nothing. I may dole out all I possess, or even give my body to be burnt, but if I have no love, I am none the better.

"Love is patient; love is kind and envies no one. Love is never boastful, nor conceited, nor rude; never selfish, not quick to take offence. Love keeps no score of wrongs; does not gloat over other men's sins, but delights in the truth. There is nothing love cannot face; there is no limit to its faith, its hope, and its endurance" (NEB).

The Charge to the Congregation and the Couple

MINISTER   On this occasion _____ and _____ come before family, friends, and church to affirm the choice that they have made of each other as life mates. They declared their intention to establish a home for the raising of a family and the fulfillment of life together. How like the Church in its relationship to its Lord is the wedding of two people. May you see in this relationship of Christ and His Church the pattern of love and devotion for husband and wife.

The Service of the Engagement Vows

MINISTER   In olden days the engagement service was performed on the church steps at the time of the announcement of the engagement of the couple. Later it was incorporated into the actual wedding service. In order to allow the bride and groom to go together to the altar, this portion of the service will be performed at the end of the main aisle opposite the altar. (MINISTER *moves to the end of aisle and is met there by the* BRIDE *and* GROOM *with* PARENTS *and* WEDDING PARTY.)

MINISTER _____ (GROOM), will you take this woman as your wife, will you be faithful to her in tender love and honor, offering her encouragement and companionship; and will you live with her, and cherish her, as love and respect would lead you, in the bond of marriage?

GROOM   I will.

MINISTER _____ (BRIDE), will you take this man as your husband; and will you honor and respect him, will you give him strength and encouragement, will you love him and live with him as a mate, a companion, and a lover, and will you faithfully cherish him in the bonds of marriage?

BRIDE   I will.

MINISTER   Who gives this woman to marry this man?

FATHER OF BRIDE   Her mother and father do.

(*Having publicly declared their intention of marriage,* THE COUPLE *and the* WEDDING PARTY *will now proceed up the main aisle to the altar.*)

Meditation

MINISTER _____ and _____, as you contemplate the making of your vows to each other, realize that henceforth your destinies shall be woven of one design and your perils and your joys shall not be known apart. Today you are making public, for all to know, that the words "I love you," are a full commitment of yourselves to each other, to the forsaking of all other lovers, and to the assuming of adult responsibility in society. Marriage has possibilities of failure and success as well as pain and joy, sorrow and happiness. The possibilities are greater in married life than in single life. You have declared your intention to make this venture of faith and love.

The Exchange of Wedding Vows

GROOM   I, _____, having full confidence that our abiding faith in each other as human beings will last our lifetime, take you, _____, to be my wedded wife; I promise to be your loving and faithful husband; in prosperity and in need, in joy and in sorrow, in sickness and in health, and to respect your privileges as an individual as long as we both shall live.

BRIDE   I, _____, having full confidence that our abiding faith in each other as human beings will last our lifetime, take you, _____, to be my wedded husband; I promise to be your loving and faithful wife; in prosperity and need, in joy and in sorrow, in sickness and in health, and wherever you go I will follow, and where you live, I will live, your people shall be my people.

The Service of the Rings (*spoken by both in double ring ceremony*)   As this ring has no end, neither shall my love for you.

THE WEDDING PRAYER (MINISTER)   Eternal God, the spring of life and giver of spiritual grace; bless these our friends, that living together, they may fulfill the vows and covenant made between them. May they ever remain in perfect love and peace together according to Your Spirit in Jesus Christ, our Lord. *Amen.*

THE LORD'S PRAYER (*in unison*)   Our Father, who art in heaven, hallowed be Thy name. Thy kingdom come, Thy will be done, on earth as it is in heaven. Give us this day our daily bread. And forgive us our debts, as we forgive our debtors. And lead us not into temptation, but deliver us from evil. For Thine is the kingdom and the power and the glory, for ever. *Amen.*

The Declaration of Marriage

MINISTER   Since you have promised your love to each other, and before God and these witnesses have exchanged these solemn vows, as a minister of Jesus, I declare you to be husband and wife. What God has joined, let no one separate.

The Benediction

MINISTER   May the joy and peace which only God can give, and which cannot be taken away by anything in this world, be yours today and in all of life's tomorrows. *Amen.*

THE RECESSIONAL HYMN   "Now Thank We All Our God" (*the*

CONGREGATION *standing and singing*)
THE POSTLUDE
Hymn to Joy   Beethoven

BLESSING OF A CIVIL MARRIAGE[15]

The minister, satisfied that the persons seeking this blessing have been lawfully married, shall say:

Dearly beloved, we are met here in the presence of God to invoke the blessings of the Heavenly Father upon your marriage. Let us reverently bring to remembrance that marriage was instituted by God for the comfort and help of his children and that families might be trained in goodness and godliness of life. Both by His presence and His solemn words, Christ honored and sanctioned it; and it is set forth and commended in the Scripture as honorable to all who enter it lawfully, seriously, and with true affection.

The minister then, asking the man to take the right hand of the woman in his right hand, shall say:

_____, do you before God and these witnesses acknowledge this woman to be your lawful wedded wife; and do you promise that from this day forward you will be her faithful husband, for better for worse, for richer for poorer, in sickness and in health, to love and to cherish, till death do you part?

The man shall answer:

I do.

The minister then, asking the woman to take the right hand of the man in her right hand, shall say:

_____, do you before God and these witnesses acknowledge this man to be your lawful wedded husband; and do you promise that from this day forward you will be his faithful wife, for better for worse, for richer for poorer, in sickness and in health, to love and to cherish, till death do you part?

The woman shall answer:

I do.

If a ring be provided, the minister, upon receiving it, shall give it to the man, requesting him, as he places it upon the fourth finger of the woman's left hand, to say:

In pledge of the vow made between us, I give you this ring; in the name of the Father, and of the Son, and of the Holy Spirit. *Amen.*

Then the minister shall say:

Let us pray. O eternal God, Creator and Preserver of all mankind, Giver of all spiritual grace, the Author of everlasting life: Send Thy blessing upon these Thy servants, this man and this woman, whom we bless in Thy name; that they, living faithfully together, may surely perform and keep the vow and convenant between them made, and may ever remain in perfect love and peace together, and live according to Thy laws, through Jesus Christ our Lord. *Amen.*

Then the minister shall say:

Inasmuch as you _____, and you _____, have covenanted to live together in holy marriage, I declare you to be husband and wife.

The bride and groom, kneeling to receive the benediction, the minister shall say:

God the Father, God the Son, God the Holy Spirit, bless, preserve, and keep you; the Lord mercifully with His favor look upon you, and fill you with all spiritual benediction and grace; that you may so live togther in this life, that in the world to come you may have life everlasting. *Amen.*

Section 5

THE FUNERAL SERVICE

The Christian Goes Home

For a Person of Advanced Age

For an Outstanding Christian

Modern Funeral Service

Funeral Service For a Child

Appropriate Scriptures

General Prayers

THE CHRISTIAN GOES HOME

The minister is on the front line of the grief-suffering experience. He belongs to the "caretaking group," along with the funeral director and physician. The minister, however, more than others, is the "chief grief therapist" through his presence, counsel, attitude, friendship, and spiritual leadership.

The pastor sees firsthand the psychological and physical reactions to death. His understanding and counsel regarding guilt, hostility, loneliness, fear, and other emotional symptoms make a difference in how family members assimilate their grief. The minister's alertness to destructive behavior plus his long-range follow-through gives him a unique opportunity.

The content of the funeral service is all important. The funeral should deal with death realistically, aid in recalling memories of the deceased, and help people to become free from guilt or self-condemnation. The funeral should demonstrate the Christian faith as a resource of comfort by presenting the love of God, the assurance of a tomorrow, and directing of attention beyond the death of the loved one. The funeral should be warm, personal, and sensitive; encouraging friends to give the bereaved the courage and support to face the responsibilities of the future. (*Minister will use appropriate pronouns—he/she—for the deceased in the services.*)

FOR A PERSON OF ADVANCED AGE

Prelude
  "Rock of Ages"
  "Peace, Perfect Peace"
  "One Sweetly Solemn Thought"

Opening Scriptural Sentence

"Lord, thou hast been our dwelling place in all generations. Before the mountains were brought forth, or ever thou hadst formed the earth and the world, even from everlasting to everlasting thou art God" (Psalms 90:1, 2).

Invocation

Merciful Father, who art Strength to the weak, Refreshment to the weary, Comfort to the sad, Help to the tempted, and Life to the dying: make us, we pray Thee, sensitive to the presence of Thy comfort in accordance with our Lord's assurance that we will not be left alone, and grant us the faith of the prophets who could see, in approaching the shades of night, the promise of glorious sunrise through Jesus Christ, our Lord. *Amen.*

Hymn (Optional) "For All the Saints Who From Their Labors Rest"

(This may be organ music, choral anthem, vocal solo, or spoken)

> For all the saints, who from their labors rest,
> Who Thee by faith before the world confessed,
> Thy name, O Jesus, be forever blessed.
> > Alleluia!
>
> Thou wast their rock, their fortress, and their might;
> Thou, Lord, their captain in the well-fought fight;
> Thou, in the darkness drear, the one true light.
> > Alleluia!
>
> O blest communion, fellowship divine.
> We feebly struggle; they in glory shine;
> Yet all are one in Thee, for all are Thine.
> > Alleluia!
>
> The golden evening brightens in the west;
> Soon, soon to faithful warriors cometh rest;
> Sweet is the calm of Paradise, the blest.
> > Alleluia!

WILLIAM W. HOWE

(Other appropriate hymn: "When on My Day of Life")

Scripture Reading

"I lift up my eyes to the hills. From whence does my help come? My help comes from the Lord, who made heaven and earth. He will not let your foot be moved, he who keeps you will not slumber. Behold, he who keeps Israel will neither slumber nor sleep. The Lord is your keeper; the Lord is your shade on your right hand. The sun shall not smite you by day, nor the moon by night. The Lord will keep you from all evil; he will keep your life. The Lord will keep your going out and your coming in from this time forth and for evermore" (Psalm 121).

"Who shall separate us from the love of Christ? Shall tribulation, or distress, or persecution, or famine, or nakedness, or peril, or sword? . . . No, in all these things we are more than conquerors through him who loved us. For I am sure that neither death, nor life, nor angels, nor principalities, nor things present, nor things to come, nor powers, nor height, nor depth, nor anything else in all creation, will be able to separate us from the love of God in Christ Jesus our Lord" (Romans 8:35, 37–39).

Prayer

Almighty God, who art like the sky that bends above us, and surrounds all the earth; who art the true and lasting light which shines even in the times of our shadow and darkness; look upon Thy children with constant mercy, and give us a spirit of understanding promised by Thy dear Son. When our eyes no longer behold what we have loved, and when we listen for footsteps of those who have gone from our sight and hear them not, we can but turn to Thee.

We thank Thee for this life which has come to its final change. May it still be an inspiration and guide. May these who have been loved by *her* keep in mind that they must love and serve Thee more because *she* is not here. May they show their love for *her* by doing things *she* loved the best. May they be gentler, kinder, more thoughtful, thus to compensate for *her* loss.

Help us to be grateful for Thine eternal love, which summons souls to rest from their labors and dost permit them at eventide to enter into Thy peace. Amid the changes of this world, make us strong and calm, eager to serve, more inclined to love, and persuade us that neither death nor life, nor things present, nor things to come, shall be able to separate us from the love of God which is in Christ Jesus our Lord. *Amen.*

Hymn (Optional)   "Abide With Me"
(This may be organ music, choral anthem, vocal solo, or spoken)

Abide with me; fast falls the eventide;
The darkness deepens; Lord, with me abide;
When other helpers fail, and comforts flee,
Help of the helpless, O abide with me.

Swift to its close ebbs out life's little day;
Earth's joys grow dim, its glories pass away;
Change and decay in all around I see;
O Thou, who changest not, abide with me.

I need Thy presence every passing hour;
What but Thy grace can foil the tempter's power?
Who like Thyself my guide and stay can be?
Through cloud and sunshine, O abide with me.

Hold Thou Thy cross before my closing eyes;
Shine through the gloom, and point me to the skies;
Heaven's morning breaks, and earth's vain shadows flee;
In life, in death, O Lord, abide with me.

HENRY F. LYTE

Meditation

THE BEAUTY OF THE SUNSET

Have you ever sat on a hill and watched the sun going down—and has your soul thrilled at the beauty of the sunset? That is what I want you to see in this death today. I like to think of this world as a park filled with gardens and playgrounds, trees and lakes, museums and swimming pools. We

are like children privileged to spend a day in the great park.
The time we are privileged to spend is not the same in length,
in light, or in beauty. Some days are long and sunlit, others
are cloudy and stormy, as in a winter's tale. Some children are
able to stay only a few short hours. Some must go home at
noon of day, while the sun is still shining. Others stay till the
sun begins to set in the beauty of the west. For each of us the
moment comes when the great nurse, Death, takes us by the
hand and quietly says, "It is time to go home, my child; come,
come with me." This one has been privileged to live until the
shadows of the setting sun had lengthened, and the evening
had come; the business of the world was hushed, and the fever
of life was over, and work was done. Oh, the beauty of the
sunset of a life like this.

Select One of the Following

1

It is a beautiful death, because it climaxes a wonderful life.
One need not eulogize the character of the departed to you
who have known *her*—*her* life tells its own story. The friendships expressed here demonstrate *her* influence; *her* family tells
something about the quality of life.

Some there are who come to the end of life filled with remorse and regret. "Take my wasted years," said one, "and
bury them with me." He had misused his life, had furthered no
great cause of human welfare, had buried his talents in cheap,
selfish security. To such the Master said, "Thou wicked and
slothful servant," and instructed that they be cast into outer
darkness.

The sweetest words which one could ever hear, the most
beautiful benediction that could conclude a life, the most cov-
eted epitaph that could grace one's farewell, would be those
words spoken by the Master when He said, "Well done, thou
good and faithful servant: thou hast been faithful over a few
things, I will make thee ruler over many things: enter thou into
the joy of thy Lord."

The one we honor lived a useful, devoted, unselfish life. The world has been made better for *her* having lived. The Kingdom of heaven has been strengthened by *her* efforts. Surely, the congratulatory hand of life's all-wise Judge reaches out to the accompaniment, "Well done, thou good and faithful servant."

2

This is a beautiful death also, because it comes as a friend to old age. I really mean that. We often wish in a childish way that life would never end, and in our rebellious moments we wonder why God created the universe so death comes at all. We feel death is an enemy of life—and not a friend.

But that is not right. It is the knowledge that our years are limited that makes them so precious. Plato was right when he declared that infinite life on this earth for us human beings would not be desirable even if it were possible. Who would want to live a never-ending existence on earth through endless years of struggle and revolution, pain and worry, conflict and labor—with no possibility of escape? Life would be so monotonous and boring with no heights or depths, without crescendos or diminuendos, with no challenge or achievement. What drudgery if day would never end, and the sun would never set.

Have you toiled through the hot, sweaty, sweltering day, looking forward to the sunset? Time moved so slowly; it seemed the day would never end. Then, when evening finally came—how welcome, what cool peace and embracing rest; what satisfying release, what a wonderful friend.

This one has lived many years, and death must have come as a friend indeed.

3

*Then, this is a beautiful death because there are rays of prom-
ise for a better tomorrow.*

> O happy soul, be thankful now, and rest!
> Heaven is a goodly land;
> And God is love; and those He loves are blest;

> Now thou dost understand
> The least thou hast is better than the best
> That thou didst hope for; now upon thine eyes
> The new life opens fair;
> Before thy feet the blessed journey lies
> Through homelands everywhere;
> And heaven to thee is all a sweet surprise.
>
> WASHINGTON GLADDEN

The best is yet to be. Death is not the end; it is only a new beginning. It is going to bed on a cold, black night, and waking with the sun always shining.

Victor Hugo, the French author, wrote, "When I go down to the grave, I can say, like many others, 'I have finished my day's work.' But I cannot say, 'I have finished my life.' My day's work will begin the next morning. The tomb is not a blind alley; it is a thoroughfare. It closes on the twilight, and opens on the dawn."

Rev. Robert J. Burdette, shortly before his death, wrote a personal letter to the editor of an Eastern paper, saying: "I watch the sunset as I look out over the rim of the blue Pacific, and there is no mystery beyond the horizon line, because I know what there is over there. I have been there. I have journeyed in those lands. Over there where the sun is sinking is Japan. That star is rising over China. In that direction lie the Philippines. I know all that. Well, there is another land that I look toward as I watch the sunset. I have never seen it. I have never seen anyone who has been there, but it has a more abiding reality than any of these lands which I know. This land beyond the sunset, this land of immortality, this fair and blessed country of the soul—why, this heaven of ours is the one thing in the world which I know with absolute, unshaken, unchangeable certainty. This I know with a knowledge that is never shadowed by a passing cloud of doubt. I may not always be certain about this world; my geographical locations may sometimes become confused, but the other world—that I know. And as the afternoon sun sinks lower, faith shines more clearly and hope, lifting her voice in a higher key, sings the songs of fruition. My work is about ended, I think. The best of it I have done poorly; any of it I might have done better, but I have done it. And in a fairer land, with finer material, and a better working light, I will do better work."[16]

> Sunset and evening star,
>> And one clear call for me!
> And may there be no moaning of the bar,
>> When I put out to sea.
>
> But such a tide as moving seems asleep,
>> Too full for sound and foam,
> When that which drew from out the boundless deep
>> Turns again home.
>
> Twilight and evening bell,
>> And after that the dark!
> And may there be no sadness of farewell,
>> When I embark;
>
> For tho' from out our bourne of Time and Place
>> The flood may bear me far,
> I hope to see my Pilot face to face
>> When I have crossed the bar.

TENNYSON

Benediction

O Lord, support us all the day long of our troublous life until the shadows lengthen and the evening comes, and the busy world is hushed, and the fever of life is over, and our work is done. Then in Thy mercy grant us a safe lodging and a holy rest, and peace at the last. *Amen.*[17]

Postlude

"Now the Day Is Over"

FOR AN OUTSTANDING CHRISTIAN

Prelude

"Largo" (Dvorak)
"Ten Thousand Times Ten Thousand"

Opening Scriptural Sentence

"Jesus said to her, 'I am the resurrection and the life; he who believes in me, though he die, yet shall he live, and whoever lives and believes in me shall never die . . .' " (John 11:25, 26).

Invocation

O God, the Lord of life, the Conqueror over death, the Repose of the faithful, our help in every time of trouble: to Thee we lift our thoughts and voices in adoration and praise in the name of Jesus Christ, who taught us how to pray saying (*unison*)

> Our Father who art in heaven,
> Hallowed be Thy name.
> Thy kingdom come,
> Thy will be done,
> On earth as it is in heaven.
> Give us this day our daily bread;
> And forgive us our debts,
> As we also have forgiven our debtors;
> And lead us not into temptation,
> But deliver us from evil.
> For Thine is the kingdom, and the power,
> And the glory, forever. *Amen.*

"Gloria Patri" (Congregation)

Hymn (optional)   "Blessed Assurance"

(This may be sung by congregation, or as a solo.)

> Blessed assurance, Jesus is mine!
> O what a foretaste of glory, divine!
> Heir of salvation, purchased of God,
> Born of His spirit, washed in His blood.

> *Chorus:*
> This is my story, this is my song,
> Praising my Saviour, all the day long;
> This is my story, this is my song,
> Praising my Saviour all the day long.

Perfect submission, perfect delight,
Visions of rapture now burst on my sight.
Angels descending, bring from above
Echoes of mercy, whispers of love.

Perfect submission, all is at rest,
I in my Saviour am happy and blest,
Watching and waiting, looking above,
Filled with His goodness, lost in His love.

FANNY J. CROSBY

Scripture Reading

The Lord is my shepherd, I shall not want; he makes me lie down in green pastures. He leads me beside still waters; he restores my soul. He leads me in paths of righteousness for his name's sake. Even though I walk through the valley of the shadow of death, I fear no evil; for thou art with me; thy rod and thy staff, they comfort me. Thou preparest a table before me in the presence of my enemies; thou anointest my head with oil, my cup overflows. Surely goodness and mercy shall follow me all the days of my life; and I shall dwell in the house of the Lord for ever (Psalm 23).

Let not your hearts be troubled; believe in God, believe also in me. In my Father's house are many rooms; if it were not so, would I have told you that I go to prepare a place for you? And when I go and prepare a place for you, I will come again and will take you to myself, that where I am you may be also (John 14:1-3).

For this perishable nature must put on the imperishable, and this mortal nature must put on immortality. When the perishable puts on the imperishable, and the mortal puts on immortality, then shall come to pass the saying that is written: "Death is swallowed up in victory." "O death, where is thy victory? O death, where is thy sting?" The sting of death is sin, and the power of sin is the law. But thanks be to God, who gives us the victory through our Lord Jesus Christ. Therefore, my beloved brethren, be steadfast, immovable, always abounding in the work of the Lord, knowing that in the Lord your labor is not in vain (1 Corinthians 15:53–58).

Bless the Lord, O my soul, and forget not all his benefits, who forgives all your iniquity, who heals all your diseases, who redeems your life from the Pit, who crowns you with steadfast love and mercy (Psalms 103:2–4).

Prayer

O God who art the strength of Thy saints and who redeemest the souls of Thy servants: we bless Thy name for all those who have died in the Lord, and who now rest from their labors, having received the end of their faith, even the salvation of their souls. Especially we call to remembrance Thy loving kindness and Thy tender mercies to this Thy servant. For all Thy goodness that withheld not *his* portion in the joys of this earthly life, and for Thy guiding hand along the way of *his* pilgrimage, we give Thee thanks and praise. Especially we bless Thee for Thy grace that kindled in *his* heart the love of Thy dear name; that enabled *him* to fight the good fight unto the end, and to obtain the victory; yea, to become more than conqueror, through Him that loveth us. We magnify Thy holy name that *his* trials and temptations being ended, sickness and death being passed, with all the dangers and difficulties of this mortal life, *his* spirit is at home in Thy presence, at whose right hand dwelleth eternal peace. And grant, O Lord, we beseech Thee, that we who rejoice in the triumph of Thy saints may profit by their example, that becoming followers of their faith and patience, we also may enter with them into an inheritance incorruptible and undefiled, and that fadeth not away. Through Jesus Christ, our Lord. *Amen.*[18]

Meditation

THANK GOD FOR EVERY REMEMBRANCE

Dear friends: We have come together today for three distinct purposes.

First, we have come to express our mutual appreciation for the life of _____. Death depreciates life, and all too often our comrades are soon forgotten. Fittingly therefore, as a company of friends, we gathered to pay honest tribute, genuine appreciation, and to think upon *his* good qualities. Our departed *brother* had many noble and commendable characteristics. All of us have a sense of loss and feel a mutual sorrow. I do not mean to imply that our *brother* was perfect; the world has known only One such person. Nor am I here determining *his* destiny. Rather, in the words of the Apostle Paul, "Whatever is true, whatever is honorable, whatever is just, whatever is pure, whatever is lovely, whatever is gracious, if there is any excellence, if there is anything worthy of praise, think about these things" (Philippians 4:8). To his friend Philemon, the Apostle wrote, "I thank my God always when I remember you ..." (Philemon 3). Just so, we lift to God our gratitude for every remembrance of our departed.

We have come here, secondly, to unify and convey our sympathetic understanding to the bereaved family. Death is a separator that drops a curtain of silence between loved ones and friends. But today we are drawn together in a company to express our sympathy, to give strength and comfort to the distressed, and to make it known that we remember with loving concern.

The old Greeks, in whose language our New Testament was written, discovered that if a person really cared about the circumstances of his fellows, he might enter vicariously into that person's experience. They called this *synpathos,* meaning "with suffering," from which comes our word *sympathy.* By means of sympathy we enter into the minds and hearts of those who suffer, to share this sorrow. The old Romans, in whose Latin language most of the history of the early Church was written, discovered that when sympathy was sincere, a miracle resulted in the bereaved. They called it *con-fortis,* meaning "together strong," and from it comes our word *comfort.*

Our sincere sympathy we extend together. May it bring the

family comfort. Often I have heard folks say, "We could not have gone through it without the support of our friends."

> My greatest joy on earth shall be,
> To find at the turning of every road,
> The strong hand of a comrade kind,
> To help me onward with my load.
>
> But since I have no gold to give
> And only love can make amends,
> My daily prayer in life shall be,
> "God make me worthy of my friends."
>
> AUTHOR UNKNOWN

However, when human strength comes to an end, you are never alone, for there is an invisible companion, a Heavenly Father, who promises, "My peace I leave with you. . . ."

Finally, we have come to reaffirm our belief in immortality. "It is the end of life for which the first was made." "Without immortality, nothing is intelligible; with immortality, everything is." Life does not end at the grave! This is the great affirmation of the Christian faith! ". . . if our earthly house of this tabernacle were dissolved, we have a building of God, an house not made with hands, eternal in the heavens. . . ." "In my Father's house are many mansions. . . ." Thanks be unto "our Savior Jesus Christ who . . . brought life and immortality to light. . . ." Death is not what we have thought it to be at all. It is closing the door to earth and opening the door to heaven. It is putting off an old suit and dressing in a beautiful new garment. Death is going to sleep on a cold, wintry night and waking to find the sun always shining.

An anxious person once asked Bishop Berggrav of Norway for an explanation of death. The Bishop told this story in reply: "One day a peasant took his little son with him on a visit to a village some distance away. Along the road they came to a swift stream which was spanned by a rickety old bridge. But it was daylight and the father and son made the crossing without mishap. . . . It was dusk when the two started their homeward journey. The boy remembered the stream and the old bridge, and became frightened. How would they be able to cross that turbulent water in the dark? His father, noticing his anxiety, lifted him up, and carried him in his arms. The fear subsided immediately, and before the boy knew it he was fast asleep on his father's shoulder.... As the sun of a new day streamed through the window of his bedroom, the boy awoke and discovered that he was safe at home."[19] Death is like that. What we fear most, the river of death, we cross unafraid if we fall asleep in Jesus. Then we shall awake in our Father's house of many mansions, where there is no night and no fear.

Choral Anthem
"Hallelujah Chorus"

Benediction
Now our Lord Jesus Christ himself, and God, even our Father, which hath loved us, and hath given us everlasting consolation and good hope through grace, Comfort your hearts and establish you in every good word and work (2 Thessalonians 2:16, 17, KJV).

Postlude
"I Know That My Redeemer Liveth," from Handel's "Messiah"

"The Heavens Declare His Glory," Beethoven

MODERN FUNERAL SERVICE

Prelude Music

Introductory Sentences   Someone very dear to all of us here has died. We are saddened because the separation seems so final. We recount now the years of joy, the associations in laughter, work, family, and service.

> Bless the Lord, O my soul,
>   and forget not all his benefits ... (Psalms 103:2).

Affirmation of Faith   Our faith is affirmed in the words of Jesus: "I am the living bread which came down from heaven; if anyone eats of this bread he will live for ever . . ." (John 6:51). ". . . I am the resurrection and the life; he who believes in me, though he die, yet shall he live . . ." (11:25). ". . . I am the way and the truth and the life; no one comes to the Father but by me. If you had known me, you would have known my Father also . . ." (14:6).

And Paul boldly affirmed, "If it is for this life only that Christ has given us hope, we of all men are most to be pitied" (1 Corinthians 15:19 NEB). "As in Adam all die, so also in Christ shall all be made alive" (1 Corinthians 15:22).

Invocation   Father God, Your infinite love was made manifest in the cross, and Your infinite power was demonstrated in the Resurrection; grant Your holy comfort to abide with these, our dear bereaved friends, until the day is over. May Your promise find fulfillment for our departed one, through Jesus Christ, who taught us to pray:

Unison (The Lord's Prayer):   Our Father in heaven; holy be Your name. Your Kingdom come, Your will be done, on earth as in heaven. Give us today our daily bread. Forgive us our sins, as we forgive those who sin against us. Save us from the time of trial, and deliver us from evil. For yours is the Kingdom, the power and the glory forever. *Amen.*

Meditation   Death is not what we have thought it to be. It is the step from transient to permanent, from temporary to eternal.

From the caterpillar emerges the butterfly;

From the grain blossoms the full blown sheath;

From the child, the adolescent is born. So in death, the years of training are over, so that the eternal work may start. The last rehearsal is finished, so that the play may begin. One class of school is graduated, so that another degree may commence.

O death—grotesque character, horror of children, foe of the fearful—take off your mask! You terrify the world. You frighten and deceive men. You bring sorrow with separation. Your sting is great.

Yet, your reason for happening is to open the door of escape from one room to give entrance to another. You are not able to take from us those that we love.

But where are they, those that we have loved? Are they in ecstasy, taken up in holy fellowship? Are they tormented in the night, burning with frustration and anxiety? Are they in lonely despair, because they loved not God?

Not at all! With what they left this life, they begin the new existence. Our eyes cannot see them because they have left their bodies for a time, as one steps out of his clothing.

However, in the Lord, we never lose our own. We know they live eternally in the spirit eternal. They are vividly present in the presence of love. We meet them when we meet the Lord. We receive them when we receive the Lord. O loved ones, eternally alive, help us to learn in this short life how to live eternally through the quality of love.

Benediction   Now let faith and hope abide because we have drunk deeply of your love, O God.

Postlude   "I Have Found Your Love in This Place"

Additional Meditation

Friends, God alone understands the sense of loss which you here have sustained in the death of _____. So let us pray to Him. O God, whom we do not know as we would like, yet whom we acknowledge as the source of all life and the sustainer beyond death; we do not ask for escape from our grief and sorrow. We pray only for a renewed faith in the reality of the unseen, and the promises of Jesus who brought life, hope, and immortality to light. *Amen.*

I do not want you to think of this so much as a "funeral service" but as a memorial and tribute to _____. We recall with tender appreciation our personal associations with him (or her). Each of us will recall different details of laughter, work, school, family, recreation, conversations, experiences, and services for which we are especially thankful.

May you who feel this loss most profoundly, find comfort, meaning, and hope in these testimonies from sacred Scripture: "The Lord is my Shepherd, I shall not want. . . . Even though I walk through the valley of the shadow of death, I fear no evil; for thou art with me; thy rod and thy staff, they comfort me" (Psalms 23:1, 4). "Let not your hearts be troubled; believe in God, believe also in me. In my Father's house are many rooms; if it were not so, would I have told you that I go to prepare a place for you? And when I go and prepare a place for you, I will come again and will take you to myself, that where I am you may be also" (John 14:1–3). ". . . and death shall be no more, neither shall there be mourning nor crying nor pain any more, for the former things have passed away" (Revelation 21:4).

Let us pray: O Father of Mercy, we tenderly thank You for this life we have loved so much. Forgive our sins of omission and commission. Relieve our feelings of remorse. We commend _____ to Thy keeping, believing in Thy eternal love and the power of resurrection through Jesus Christ. O Blessed Hope! O Blessed Peace! All is well through Jesus Christ. *Amen.*

We are never more a community in Christ than in these moments, for we dare to gather in the face of death and proclaim the word, dry weeping eyes, declare our mutual dependence and celebrate.

In the large perspective, we do gather here for celebration. Not celebration that death has come, but that God is God, the Father and sustainer of the Jesus-like life and spirit. Our celebration is not centered in some guarantee or specific prediction of what happens to us after death. We simply give ourselves and our dead into the hands of One whose love is the only certainty that lies beyond our fragile forecast. We know that in death as in life we are in Him, and that is enough to know. "We know that in everything God works for good with those

who love him, who are called according to his purpose"
(Romans 8:28).

We go forth to continue living in the certainty that life and
death are gracious gifts from God who fills both of them with
meaning.

"Let us then with confidence draw near to the throne of
grace, that we may receive mercy and find grace to help in time
of need" (Hebrews 4:16). "It is the Lord who goes before you;
he will be with you, he will not fail you or forsake you; do not
fear or be dismayed" (Deuteronomy 31:8). "He only is my rock
and my salvation . . ." (Psalms 62:2).

O God—a very precious person has left our midst. We are
glad for the glow of faith and hope that rises in our hearts
through the knowledge of Jesus Christ, who verified that love
is stronger than hate, that life outlasts death, and who assured
us, saying, ". . . because I live, you will live also" (John 14:19).
Glory be to Thee. *Amen.*

FUNERAL SERVICE FOR A CHILD

Organ Prelude

> "O God, Our Help in Ages Past"
> "The King of Love My Shepherd Is"
> "Lead, Kindly Light"

Opening Scriptural Sentence

"The eternal God is your dwelling place, and underneath
are the everlasting arms" (Deuteronomy 33:27).

"To thee, O Lord, I lift up my soul. . . . Turn thou to me, and
be gracious to me; for I am lonely and afflicted. Relieve the
troubles of my heart, and bring me out of my distresses. Consider my affliction and my trouble, and forgive all my sins"
(Psalms 25:1, 16–18).

Hymn (optional) "Saviour, Like a Shepherd Lead Us"

(This may be organ music, choral anthem, vocal solo, or
spoken.)

Saviour, like a shepherd lead us,
   Much we need Thy tender care;
In Thy pleasant pastures feed us,
   For our use Thy folds prepare:
Blessed Jesus, Blessed Jesus!
   Thou has bought us, Thine we are,
Blessed Jesus, Blessed Jesus!
   Thou hast bought us, Thine we are.

Thou hast promised to receive us,
   Poor and sinful tho' we be;
Thou hast mercy to relieve us,
   Grace to cleanse, and power to free:
Blessed Jesus, Blessed Jesus!
   Early let us turn to Thee,
Blessed Jesus, Blessed Jesus!
   Early let us turn to Thee.

Early let us seek Thy favor,
   Early let us do Thy will;
Blessed Lord and only Saviour,
   With Thy love our bosoms fill:
Blessed Jesus, Blessed Jesus!
   Thou hast loved us, love us still,
Blessed Jesus, Blessed Jesus!
   Thou hast loved us, love us still.

DOROTHY A. THRUPP

(Other appropriate selections: "Brightly Gleams Our Banner"; "He Shall Feed His Flock"; "O Love That Wilt Not Let Me Go"; "Angel Voices, Ever Singing.")

Scripture Reading

At that time the disciples came to Jesus, saying, "Who is the greatest in the kingdom of heaven?" And calling to him a child, he put him in the midst of them, and said, "Truly, I say to you, unless you turn and become like children, you will never enter the kingdom of heaven" (Matthew 18:1-3).

. . . for to such belongs the kingdom of heaven (Matthew 19:14).

Thus says the Lord: "A voice is heard in Ramah, lamentation and bitter weeping. Rachel is weeping for her children; she refuses to be comforted for her children, because they are not." Thus says the Lord: "Keep your voice from weeping, and your eyes from tears; for your work shall be rewarded, says the Lord ..." (Jeremiah 31:15, 16).

And the streets of the city shall be full of boys and girls playing in its streets (Zechariah 8:5).

They shall hunger no more, neither thirst any more; the sun shall not strike them, nor any scorching heat. For the Lamb in the midst of the throne will be their shepherd, and he will guide them to springs of living water; and God will wipe away every tear from their eyes (Revelation 7:16, 17).

Prayer

O God of love and mercy, we thank Thee that Thou art able to comfort these parents whose joy has been turned into sorrow, whose house has been left desolate by the passing of this little one. We thank Thee for the assurance that their loved one is at rest in Thee and that love can never lose its own. Let the things unseen and eternal grow more real, more present, more full of meaning and power. Let Thy strength sustain their weakness. Free them from any bitterness and fill them with Thy peace, through Jesus Christ our Lord. *Amen.*

Meditation

STARGAZING IN THE NIGHT

A little girl was impressed by the stars. She had many questions to ask concerning them. "Are the stars there all the time? Why can't you see them during the day?" Her mother replied, "You can see them only at night. Darkness is always more beautiful if we will look up at the stars rather than into the corners of blackness."[20]

That is what I want us to do today—to go stargazing. We sit in the shadow of a black night of sorrow and grief; and yet we sit in the light of the greatest hope the world has ever known. There are some thoughts that shine out like stars in the midnight sky. If we will fasten our minds upon them, instead of upon the darkness, they will give us comfort.

1

One cluster of stars is this: *We can be thankful rather than resentful.*

Hannah, the mother of the child Samuel, said, "For this child I prayed, and the Lord hath given me my petition which I asked of him." This child also has been the gracious gift and has brought much joy to your life. We can pause in gratitude for the years of happiness that *he* has brought to parents, grandparents, relatives, and friends.

We can be thankful too that God is able to salvage some value even out of such tragic happenings. The Scripture declares: "A little child shall lead them," and certainly this event brings the eternal value of life closer to us who are left. Rufus Jones once declared that his boy who died had been a greater influence over him than all the others.

Often the first reaction in bereavement is resentment. Some cry, "Oh, why did God do this to us? Why did God take our baby?" If we more fully understood God, His character, His ways, His purposes, we would see that not everything that happens in this world is God's doing. In fact, this world is filled with happenings that are not God's will at all. Says the Bible, "It is not the will of your Father, that one of these little ones should perish." There are evil forces and even human elements interacting upon all that happens in this world. Therefore, do not be resentful toward God because of the death of this child, rather be thankful for the privilege of *his* life and the precious memories you still have. That is a cluster of stars in the night.

2

Here is another: *Do not think too greatly of your own loss, but think of the joys of children in heaven.*

So much of our grief is self-centered. Our tears are tears of self-pity. If we will think of the glorious place to which the child has gone, it will console us. A mother of a young lad who had died wrote a friend, "I hardly know how to tell you, and I have not told you before simply because I did not have the heart to do so—that our dear boy entered his new life last month. Only the thought of his rich and wonderful experiences in these first days of his new life consoles us, or in any way makes up for the loss we feel in his absence."[21]

A similar incident is recorded in the Old Testament. The Shunammite woman had lost her child. Elisha, the prophet, sent his servant to inquire, "Is it well with thee? Is it well with thy child?" Though the child was dead, she responded, "It is well."

Yes, it is well, for God has provided a house of many mansions, a place for growing boys and girls to play. "The streets of the city shall be filled with boys and girls playing in its streets...." There your child will escape war and find everlasting peace. There no rough work will scar *his* palms; no sin shall darken *his* life. No cry of pain shall ever touch *his* lips. Look at these stars in the darkness and say:

[He] is not dead—the child of our affection—
    But gone unto that school
Where [he] no longer needs our poor protection,
    And Christ Himself doth rule.

In that great cloister's stillness and seclusion,
    By guardian angels led,
Safe from temptation, safe from sin's pollution,
    [He] lives, whom we call dead.

Day after day we think what [he] is doing
    In those bright realms of air;
Year after year, [his] tender steps pursuing,
    Behold [him] grown more fair.

Thus do we walk with [him], and keep unbroken
    The bond which nature gives,
Thinking that our remembrance, though unspoken
    May reach [him] where [he] lives.

                              HENRY WADSWORTH LONGFELLOW

Benediction

"May the God of hope fill you with all joy and peace in believing, so that by the power of the Holy Spirit you may abound in hope. *Amen*" (Romans 15:13).

Postlude

"How Firm a Foundation, Ye Saints of the Lord"
"Now Let Every Tongue Adore Thee" (J. Bach)

APPROPRIATE SCRIPTURES

Our Christian faith is made for times such as this. The Scriptures speak to our most acute personal needs with a wisdom that has been built upon the experience of untold generations who met the tribulations of life and became "more than conquerors." Listen to their testimonies of faith, and you will find renewed hope.

Glorious Assurance

"The Lord is my shepherd, I shall not want. . . . Even though I walk through the valley of the shadow of death, I fear no evil; for thou art with me; thy rod and thy staff, they comfort me" (Psalms 23:1, 4). "For this perishable nature must put on the imperishable, and this mortal nature must put on immortality. When the perishable puts on the imperishable, and the mortal puts on immortality, then shall come to pass the saying that is written: 'Death is swallowed up in victory'" (1 Corinthians 15:53, 54). ". . . neither death, nor life, nor angels, nor principalities, nor things present, nor things to come, nor powers, nor height, nor depth, nor anything else in all creation, will be able to separate us from the love of God in Christ Jesus our Lord" (Romans 8:38, 39). " 'Let not your hearts be troubled; believe in God, believe also in me. In my Father's house are many rooms; if it were not so, would I have told you that I go to prepare a place for you? And when I go and prepare a place for you, I will come again and will take you to myself, that where I am you may be also' " (John 14:1–3). ". . . and death shall be no more, neither shall there be mourning nor crying nor pain any more, for the former things have passed away" (Revelation 21:4). " 'They shall hunger no more, neither thirst any more; the sun shall not strike them, nor any scorching heat. For the Lamb in the midst of the throne will be their shepherd, and he will guide them to springs of living water; and God will wipe away every tear from their eyes' " (Revelation 7:16, 17).

Victory Over Tribulations

"God is our refuge and strength, a very present help in trouble" (Psalms 46:1). " 'When you pass through the waters I will be with you; and through the rivers, they shall not overwhelm you; when you walk through fire you shall not be burned, and the flame shall not consume you. For I am the Lord your God . . .' " (Isaiah 43:2, 3). "He said, 'The Lord is my rock, and my fortress, and my deliverer, my God, my rock, in whom I take refuge, my shield and the horn of my salvation, my stronghold and my refuge, my savior . . .' " (2 Samuel 22:2, 3). "What then shall we say to this? If God is for us, who is against us? He who did not spare his own Son but gave him up for us all, will he not also give us all things with him? Who shall bring any charge against God's elect? It is God who justifies; who is to condemn? Is it Christ Jesus, who died, yes, who was raised from the dead, who is at the right hand of God, who indeed intercedes for us? Who shall separate us from the love of Christ? Shall tribulation, or distress, or persecution, or famine, or nakedness, or peril, or sword? . . . No, in all these things we are more than conquerors through him who loved us" (Romans 8:31–35, 37). "For this slight momentary affliction is preparing for us an eternal weight of glory beyond all comparison, because we look not to the things that are seen but to the things that are unseen; for the things that are seen are transient, but the things that are unseen are eternal" (2 Corinthians 4:17, 18).

God's Provisions

"The Lord is my light and my salvation; whom shall I fear? The Lord is the stronghold of my life; of whom shall I be afraid?" (Psalms 27:1). "When I am afraid, I put my trust in thee. In God, whose word I praise, in God I trust without a fear. What can flesh do to me?" (Psalms 56:3, 4). ". . . I heard a voice from heaven saying, 'Write this: Blessed are the dead who die in the Lord henceforth.' 'Blessed indeed,' says the Spirit, 'that they may rest from their labors, for their deeds follow them!' " (Revelation 14:13). "But, as it is written, 'What no eye has seen, nor ear heard, nor the heart of man conceived, what God has prepared for those who love him' " (1 Corinthians 2:9). "Then the King will say to those at his right hand, 'Come, O blessed of my Father, inherit the kingdom prepared for you from the foundation of the world; for I was hungry and you gave me food, I was thirsty and you gave me drink, I was a stranger and you welcomed me, I was naked and you clothed me, I was sick and you visited me, I was in prison and you came to me.' . . . 'Truly, I say to you, as you did it to one of the least of these my brethren, you did it to me' " (Matthew 25:34–36, 40). "Then I saw a new heaven and a new earth; for the first heaven and the first earth had passed away, and the sea was no more. And I saw the holy city, new Jerusalem, coming down out of heaven from God, prepared as a bride adorned for her husband; and I heard a great voice from the throne saying, 'Behold, the dwelling of God is with men. He will dwell with them, and they shall be his people, and God himself will be with them . . .' " (Revelation 21:1–3). "For we know that if the earthly tent we live in is destroyed, we have a building from God, a house not made with hands, eternal in the heavens" (2 Corinthians 5:1).

The Resurrected Life

"But we would not have you ignorant, brethren, concerning those who are asleep, that you may not grieve as others do who have no hope. For since we believe that Jesus died and rose again, even so, through Jesus, God will bring with him those who have fallen asleep" (1 Thessalonians 4:13, 14). "If for this life only we have hoped in Christ, we are of all men most to be pitied. But in fact Christ has been raised from the dead, the first fruits of those who have fallen asleep" (1 Corinthians 15:19, 20). "What is sown is perishable, what is raised is imperishable. It is sown in dishonor, it is raised in glory. It is sown in weakness, it is raised in power. It is sown a physical body, it is raised a spiritual body. If there is a physical body, there is also a spiritual body. Thus it is written, 'The first man Adam became a living being'; the last Adam became a life-giving spirit" (1 Corinthians 15:42–45). "Just as we have borne the image of the man of dust, we shall also bear the image of the man of heaven. I tell you this, brethren: flesh and blood cannot inherit the kingdom of God, nor does the perishable inherit the imperishable. Lo! I tell you a mystery. We shall not all sleep, but we shall all be changed, in a moment, in the twinkling of an eye, at the last trumpet. For the trumpet will sound, and the dead will be raised imperishable, and we shall be changed. For this perishable nature must put on the imperishable, and this mortal nature must put on immortality" (1 Corinthians 15:49–53). "But thanks be to God, who gives us the victory through our Lord Jesus Christ. Therefore, my beloved brethren, be steadfast, immovable, always abounding in the work of the Lord, knowing that in the Lord your labor is not in vain" (1 Corinthians 15:57, 58).

GENERAL PRAYERS

1

O Thou who hast made no life in vain, and who lovest all that Thou hast made: we bow in gratitude for the life of the departed one in whose memory we are met. Recall to our minds the relationships which have made this life meaningful to us, and for those qualities beyond physical dimensions that we have experienced in *him*.

O Father of mercy and goodness, whose nature is love: release the feelings of remorse, with the knowledge that Thou dost love us in spite of our shortcomings, so we can love and forgive ourselves for deeds done and undone. Remove any feelings of resentment toward anyone by the memory of our Lord, who forgave and loved even those who misused and abused Him. Grant to these upon whom this death comes, the ability to face the reality of loss, to accept the fact without escape, and to assimilate it into their lives so that they can live usefully and normally, as Thou wouldst have them.

O Thou who art from everlasting to everlasting, the *Alpha* and the *Omega* of all things: Deepen our faith in Thee, O God, and in Thy provisions for life beyond death, through Jesus Christ. Support with Thy Church's fellowship, these friends, and bind the hearts of the family with the bonds of Christian love, until the morning dawns and the shadows flee away. Through Jesus Christ. *Amen.*

2

O Thou who art the Lord of Life and the Conqueror of Death: Help us to know that we are spiritual beings living in a spiritual universe, so we need not fear death. Help us to believe that while the things that are seen pass away, and that things that are unseen are real and eternal, so we need not despair. Help us to realize the new spiritual life in Christ, which death cannot take away and the grave cannot destroy. With this assurance we find comfort and peace.

O Thou Source of all good, we thank Thee for the goodness in our *brother,* for *his* experience of Thy redeeming grace, for *his* faithfulness in all relationships. The passing of every faithful spirit brings us more closely to that inheritance which is undefiled, incorruptible, and reserved in heaven for all who love Thee, through Jesus Christ. *Amen.*

3

Eternal Spirit, Father of our spirits, from whom we have come, to whom we belong, and in whose fellowship is our peace: we turn to Thee. Amid the turmoil of emotion and the loneliness of loss, remind us of all the spiritual assets that have blessed our lives. Refresh in us the first loves that made our families. Kindle anew in us the beauty of parental relationships and the ties of blood. Strengthen the bonds of our friendships which add comfort and enlarge vision. May the fellow-ship of the churches *she* has served surround *her* with a great cloud of witnesses, confirming faith and bolstering courage. When knowledge questions *why* and sight is dim, tie our faith to Jesus Christ, who opened up the shades so we can view the horizon and find the way.

4

Heavenly Father, we thank Thee for every remembrance of our departed: for the qualities of personality that endeared *her* to us all; for the unselfish service rendered to Thy Kingdom; for the *mother's* love which fortified *her* children; and for the devoted companionship in the ministry. Into Thine eternal presence we commend *her* keeping.

We pray for those upon whom this death so closely comes. May they be comforted with the same comfort wherewith we have been comforted—the knowledge that love does not lose its own; the assurance of forgiveness for neglect; the promise of a glad reunion day; and the certainty that Thou dost work in all things for good to those who love Thee, through Jesus Christ, our Lord. *Amen.*

Section 6

HOLY WEEK SERVICES

Palm Sunday

(Traditional and Contemporary)

Good Friday

(Traditional and Contemporary)

Easter

(Traditional and Contemporary)

PALM SUNDAY

TRADITIONAL SERVICE

Call to Worship

Lift up your heads, O gates! and be lifted up, O ancient doors! that the King of glory may come in. Who is this King of glory? The Lord of hosts, he is the King of glory (Psalms 24:9–10).

Invocation

Messiah of the ages, whose Spirit is forever seeking entrance into our world's life, and whose Church ever seeks to extend Thine empire over human hearts: We would open now the doors of our hearts to Thee. Forbid that we should hail Thee as Master when all men speak well of Thee, and then deny Thee in the lonely hour of rejection. Grant us in this hour glimpses of service wherein we can hasten the consummation of Thy Kingdom in which Christ shall be the only King. *Amen.*

Scripture Lessons

Psalms: 8; 15; 16:6–11; 24; 29; 102:1, 8–12.

Old Testament: Jeremiah 7:1–11; 18:1–14.

New Testament: Matthew 21:23–46. Mark 15:16–20. Luke 19:29–44. John 19:1–37.

Palm Sunday Litany

LEADER Behold thy King cometh. In His days shall the righteous flourish, and abundance of peace so long as the moon endureth. He shall have dominion from sea to sea, and from the river unto the ends of the earth.

RESPONSE Blessed is He that cometh in the name of the Lord.

147

LEADER   God has highly exalted Him, and bestowed on Him a name which is above every name; that at the name of Jesus every knee should bow in heaven and on earth and under the earth, and every tongue confess that Jesus Christ is Lord, to the glory of God the Father.

RESPONSE   Enter into His gates with thanksgiving and into His courts with praise.

Pastor's Palm Sunday Prayer

O God, whose dearly beloved Son was greeted by the crowd on Olivet with Hallelujahs, but who in that same week was mocked as He went lonely to the cross: Forbid that our praise to Him should be in words alone. Help us, we pray, to keep the road open for Him into our hearts; let Him not find in us another crucifixion—but rather love and loyalty in which His Kingdom may be established ever more.

O Christ, King of the Universe, who dost forever ride up to the gates of human lives: Open our hearts to Thy love, Thy light, Thy Spirit, that we may receive Thee as our King and never reject Thee. Enter our cities, take captive our homes, cleanse our churches of ugliness, pollution, and indifference; drive out those who traffic upon human souls; reign, O Master, till all injustice, all evil, all smallness is dethroned and destroyed.

Merciful Father: Pardon us who often close the gates of our lives against the entrance of Christ's Spirit; forgive our love of self which does not allow Him to lead us in a larger life; deliver us from ambitions and rivalries that will not allow Him to lead our homes, cities, and nation.

Save us from the hypocrisy that sings *Hosanna* in the church and cries *Crucify* in the marketplace. Save us from the sham that praises with lips but betrays in deeds. Deliver us from the treason that boasts loyalty in the upper room but makes cowardly denial in the judgment halls.

When the palms have withered, the songs are dead, and the streets empty, may we find ourselves at the end of life's little day still with Thee. *Amen.*[22]

CONTEMPORARY SERVICE

Call to Worship

"Lift up your heads, O gates! and be lifted up, O ancient doors! that the King of glory may come in.... Who is this King of glory? The Lord of hosts, he is the King of glory!" (Psalms 24:7, 10).

The voice of rejoicing and salvation is in the tabernacles of the righteous. Blessed is He that comes in the name of the Lord.

Invocation

God of truth and righteousness, we praise Thee for the Master who rode in triumph into the city of His fathers to challenge their evils. We thank Thee that Jesus came, not as a conqueror to destroy, but as a Messiah to save. In the spirit of praise and reverence, we bow and with our tongues confess that Jesus Christ is Lord, to Thy glory, O God, our Father. *Amen.*

Palm Sunday Litany

LEADER   Our Father, we take our place among the glad multitude who hail the King of kings. Stir us and our complacent nation anew because of His coming.

PEOPLE   Blessed is He that cometh in the name of the Lord.

LEADER   O God, whose dearly beloved Son was greeted by the crowd with *hallelujahs,* but who later that same week was mocked, as He followed His lonely way to the cross; forbid that our welcome to Him should be in words alone.

PEOPLE   Help us, we beseech Thee, to keep the road open for Him into our hearts.

LEADER   Most compassionate Father, send the Spirit of Thy Son, this day, to all who sit in darkness within the walled cities of their own sorrows or problems. May they hear the song of rejoicing of those who love Jesus.

PEOPLE   O Thou who has been made King and Lord of glory, enter, we pray Thee, into our hearts.[23]

Suggested Hymns   "All Hail the Power of Jesus' Name"; "All Glory, Laud, and Honor"; "Ride On! Ride On in Majesty"; "Crown Him With Many Crowns"

Suggested Scripture Readings

From the Psalms   24; 118.

Old Testament Lesson   Zechariah 9:9–14; Malachi 3:1–12.

New Testament Lesson   Matthew 21:1–17; Mark 11:1–11; Luke 19:28–40.

Pastoral Prayer

O Lord of love, who on this day long ago entered the rebellious city, confronting head-on the entrenched evils; we are grateful that Thy Spirit is forever seeking entrance into our world's life—as the impulse for fairness—as the yearning to eliminate injustice and war—as the self-giving spirit that bears other's burdens even to a cross.

O Lord, give us responsive hearts and lasting devotion, lest we be found among those who speak well of Thee when it is popular to do so, and then deny Thee when the cost is great. Increase our conviction in Jesus, we pray, so that we may be numbered among those who bear in our hands the scars of the cross and rejoice in the eternal triumphs, when every knee shall bow and every tongue confess that Thou art the King of kings and Lord of lords. *Amen.*

Offertory Sentence

"Take heed, and beware of all covetousness; for a man's life does not consist in the abundance of his possessions" (Luke 12:15).

Offertory Prayer

O Christ, King of Life, who long ago asked for the use of a donkey to enter the city, grant that we may not withhold our possessions when Thou dost say, "I have need of it." Help us to crown Thee as the Master even in our giving for Thy Kingdom's sake. *Amen.*

Suggested Anthems   "The King's Welcome" (Whitehead); "Hosanna to the Son of David" (Weelkes); "The Palms" (Faure)

Suggested Closing Hymn   "All Hail the Power of Jesus' Name"; "Ride On! Ride On in Majesty"

Benediction

"Now may the Lord of peace himself give you peace at all times in all ways. The Lord be with you all" (2 Thessalonians 3:16).

GOOD FRIDAY

TRADITIONAL SERVICE

Call to Worship

Surely he has borne our griefs and carried our sorrows . . . he was wounded for our transgressions, he was bruised for our iniquities; upon him was the chastisement that made us whole; and with his stripes we are healed. . . . Let us then with confidence draw near to the throne of grace, that we may receive mercy and find grace to help in time of need (Isaiah 53:4, 5; Hebrews 4:16).

Invocation

Almighty and most merciful God, whose will is that all men should be saved, and who didst give Thy Son our Lord Jesus Christ to be the propitiation for the sins of the whole world: We bow in adoration before Thy throne and praise Thee for this Thine unspeakable gift. *Amen.*[24]

Scripture Lessons

Psalm: 22.

Old Testament: Isaiah 53:1–12; 63:1–9.

New Testament: Matthew 27:33–55. Mark 15:16–41. Luke 23:26–49. John 19:1–37.

Good Friday Litany

LEADER   All loving and gracious God, who dost permit us to draw nigh to Thee: Dispose our hearts aright, that we may lift up prayer and praise to Thee, trusting not in our well deserving, but in Thy great mercy; through Thine only begotten Son, Jesus Christ.

RESPONSE   Bow down Thine ear, O Lord, and answer us; for we are poor and needy.

LEADER   Comfort the soul of Thy servant; for Thou, Lord, art gracious and ever ready to forgive.

RESPONSE   Bestow upon us Thy lovingkindness and Thy tender mercies, and heal us with Thy holy presence.

LEADER   That in the life of Jesus Christ our Lord, born of a woman and bearing in Himself the temptations of mortal flesh, Thou hast revealed Thine immeasurable love to us,

RESPONSE   We bless Thee, O Lord.

LEADER   That in His life and death He did not refuse to share the lot of common man, but humbled Himself and became obedient to death, even the death of the cross,

RESPONSE   We bless Thee, O Lord.

LEADER   That Thou didst not leave Thy Holy One to see corruption, but didst raise Him by the right hand of Thy power, to be to us for evermore the promise of eternal life,

RESPONSE   We bless Thee, O Lord.

LEADER   Grant that this day of holy memorial, when we recall His dying agony and His redeeming love, may be to us, His disciples, for the renewal of our faith and the sanctification of our lives,

RESPONSE   Hear us, good Lord.

LEADER   For the forgiveness of our sins and for the cleansing of our hearts,

RESPONSE   We bless Thee, O Lord.

LEADER   For that preparation of heart and mind that shall enable us to receive Thy Holy Spirit,

RESPONSE   We pray Thee, O Lord.[25]

Pastor's Good Friday Prayer

Eternal God, our Father, who didst send Thy Son to be the Saviour of the world: We wait before Thee in the shadows of the cross where He made the supreme sacrifice that lost men might find their way back to Thee. We confess that the sins which killed Him often besiege our own hearts. We see ourselves in the varied company around Him on Golgotha. We know the mood of fear, jealousy, hatred, and love of power. Search us, O God, and reveal to us our evil ways that in full surrender to Thee we may be cleansed of all that corrupts our souls and separates us from Thee. Forbid that on this day of His great agony we should join the mob that watched Him there in morbid humor and pagan cruelty. Deliver us from the passive curiosity that wants a sign and the hypocrisy that joins the crowd to hide its emptiness. May Thy Spirit find us today where we really are in our human frailty, our lagging loyalty, and our lack of faith. May the Light that overcomes the darkness touch the unseen depths of our hearts and expel all cowardice and unworthy motive. May He who came to make all things new begin in us now, and continue with each passing day, that work of redemption which shall give us the right to share in His Resurrection and make this earth at last the heaven for which He taught us to pray. *Amen.*[26]

CONTEMPORARY SERVICE

LEADER   "Is it nothing to you, all ye that pass by?"
PEOPLE   "Behold, and see if there be any sorrow like unto [His] sorrow" (Lamentations 1:12 KJV).
LEADER   "God commendeth his love toward us, in that, while we were yet sinners, Christ died for us" (Romans 5:8 KJV).
PEOPLE   "Behold the Lamb of God, who takes away the sin of the world!" (John 1:29).

or:

"He was wounded for our transgressions, he was bruised for our iniquities: the chastisement of our peace was upon him; and with his stripes we are healed" (Isaiah 53:5 KJV).

Hymns   "O Sacred Head, Now Wounded"; "Alas! And Did My Savior Bleed"

Invocation

Almighty God, our Father, in this hour of solemn remembrance, we acknowledge with sorrow and shame that our sins are such as sent our Lord to the cross. We come beseeching Thee mercifully to guide us in our meditations, supplications, and prayers and to dispose the minds and hearts of all men everywhere toward the attainment of everlasting salvation, through Jesus Christ. *Amen.*

Suggested Anthem "Lamb of God" (Haydn); or "Crucifixion" (Stainer)

The First Word
Scripture Lesson   Luke 23:32–38
Suggested Hymn   "Jesus Calls Us O'er the Tumult"; or "O Come and Mourn With Me Awhile"

Prayer

Everloving and merciful Father, who art always more ready to forgive than we are to repent, we remember this day the suffering and death of our Lord Jesus Christ, and confess to Thee our shame in the sins which crucified Him. Grant us grace that we may be reconciled to Thee, through Thy Son and our Lord. *Amen.*

Meditation Starter "The Word of Forgiveness"

This is one of the most comforting passages in all the New Testament. It reveals the magnanimous Spirit of Jesus toward His persecutors in the midst of agony. The burden of His prayer was for forgiveness for all who had a part in His Crucifixion, but in particular for those too ignorant to see what they were doing. The remarkable nature of the prayer stands out, as one considers the groups gathered around the cross. Few protested. Some sorrowed, but they sorrowed over the suffering Jesus endured; only Jesus was concerned over the tragedy of the souls who could so indifferently afflict it. It wasn't the pain inflicted upon Him that hurt so much as the stupidity and blindness. They had become accustomed to cruelty, and accepted the uncaring system.

The Second Word
Scripture Lesson   Luke 23:39–43
Suggested Hymn   "O Jesus I Have Promised"; or "Into the Woods My Master Went"

Prayer
O Thou who art love, look mercifully upon the poor, the op-pressed, and all who are victims of the suffering, injustice, and misery which stalk the earth. Fill our hearts with Christ's compassion and hasten the coming of Thy Kingdom of justice and salvation, through Jesus Christ, our Lord.

Meditation Starter   "The Word of Salvation"
The Crucifixion scene is a study in contrasts. Nowhere is this more evident than in the case of the two thieves, for the cross that stood between them thrust them worlds apart. One damned by bitterness; the other saved by hope. One cynical; the other responsive. One railed on Christ for His impo-tence; the other blessed Him for His compassion. Faced the same agonies, yet one believed he saw the mercy and au-thority of God in Jesus.

The Third Word
Scripture Lesson   John 19:25–27
Suggested Hymn   "What a Friend We Have in Jesus"; or "Near the Cross Her Vigil Keeping"

Prayer
Our God and Our Father, our Friend and Companion; grant that all the bonds of love and friendship may be made stronger and sweeter through Jesus Christ, who in His men-tal agony was not unmindful of His mother's or His disci-ple's needs, nor our need of one another's love and His supreme love. *Amen.*

Meditation Starter   "The Word of Remembrance"
This is a deeply moving scene—the compassionate thoughtfulness of One in the midst of agony to show tender concern for His mother's care. Mary had never really under-

stood her Son. She seems to have been bothered by doubts about her Son's actions and sanity. That is why Jesus commended His mother to John, rather than to His brothers and sisters. Mary needed an understanding heart. The Crucifixion was a terrible experience for her. Jesus was concerned for her soul. He wanted her to be protected by the warm fellowship of a loyal believing heart. John and Mary needed each other. The Church is our "Beloved Community."

The Fourth Word
Scripture Lesson   Mark 15:33–34
Suggested Hymn   "In the Hour of Trial"; or "Alone Thou Goest Forth, O Lord"; or " 'Tis Midnight, and on Olive's Brow"

Prayer
Almighty God, who are a tower of strength to all who put their trust in Thee, to whom all things in heaven and on earth at last must bow and surrender; even in our deepest agony help us to know and feel that we are not forsaken; that underneath are the everlasting arms; and that there is no other name under heaven given to man, in whom and through whom we may receive salvation—none but the name of Jesus Christ, Thy Son and our Lord. *Amen.*

Meditation Starter   "The Word of Loneliness"
No more poignant words have wrung from human lips than the quotation from the Twenty-second Psalm: "My God, my God, why hast thou forsaken me?" His Kingship does not take away the desperate human emotion of desolation and abandonment that He felt. His humanity was responding, as well as His divinity. Have you ever thought how lonely God must be? How lonely Jesus must have been? He thought God would transform the cross into a triumph, yet there was no sign as yet. God restrained His power to interfere and left His love in Christ to stand alone, on its own, forcing evil's worst for all the world to see. Our hearts can

trust Him who trusted love, faced death, and proved the victory.

The Fifth Word
Scripture Lesson   John 19:28, 29
Suggested Hymn   "Beneath the Cross of Jesus"; or "Deep Were His Wounds"

Prayer
God our Heavenly Father, whose most dear Son found life not a bed of roses, but suffered pain, and entered not into glory before He was crucified; save us from believing that faith will keep us from troubles, and from becoming disillusioned or bitter if trouble does come. Grant that we, walking in the way of the cross, may find from Thee the strength to meet what we must, not in despair, but in peace with Thee and ourselves, through Jesus Christ. *Amen.*

Meditation Starter   "The Word of Suffering"
This is the only word from the cross referring to Jesus' physical suffering. Crucifixion was a most horrible agony. No part of the body was free from pain. There was an intolerable craving for water. We can't explain away the suffering as the Gnostics did, saying He "thirsted for God" or He "thirsted for human souls." Suffering was *real* for Jesus. A great heresy of the Church today is not that we do not accept Jesus' deity, but are superficial in accepting His humanity. When God sought our salvation, He sought it through a *human.* The cross is very precious; it declares that in Him love had to suffer as man suffers. Only thus could He save us, not as God from without, but as God within us.

The Sixth Word
Scripture Lesson   John 19:30
Suggested Hymn   "When I Survey the Wondrous Cross"; or "Go to Dark Gethsemane"

Prayer
O God, we are thankful for the courage and devotion of Jesus in facing the cross and enduring death victoriously;

thus fulfilling Thy mission for His life, and the means of Thy redemption of the world. Increase in us true devotion to Thee, nourish us in faith, and by Thy great mercy keep us steadfast, through Jesus Christ our Lord. *Amen.*

Meditation Starter   "The Word of Triumph"

What was finished? His agony? His ordeal? His testing? His work as Messiah? His earthly destiny?

One thing is certain—He had done what God had laid upon Him to do. He had fulfilled His life's calling in thirty-three years. The redemptive work was done; salvation's opportunity for all was accomplished; the cosmic struggle was over!

Even the cross had not forced Him to capitulate to evil forces. Love was loyal to the finish. Evil was impotent to overcome the qualities of love and faith that stood up before the powers of wickedness.

The Seventh Word

Scripture Lesson   Luke 23:44–49

Suggested Hymn   "In the Cross of Christ I Glory"

Prayer

O God our Father, beyond whose love and care we can never go; we thank Thee for the assurance that Thou art the Keeper of Life even after death. When we look upon Him who was wounded for our transgressions, we are brought low, and our pride is humbled. When we remember His Spirit and faithfulness, even to death, we are inspired and, at the same time, stricken in conscience for our lack of courage and dedication. O God of mercy, uphold us by Thy strength, that in the end we may be accepted of Thee as faithful servants, in Jesus Christ our Savior. *Amen.*

Meditation Starter   "The Word of Reunion"

From one standpoint this might be the last desperate cry of a broken, defeated, dying spirit, giving up His dream. From another, it might be the final triumphant declaration of a confident faith putting His complete loyalty into the hands of the Father. There is a vast difference.

Jesus put His life into the hands of God unconditionally and let Him take Him through to the place where faith had to face the ultimate trial. It was not playacting. It was a terrifying experience. Christian discipleship calls for an adventure in love, which accepts suffering and frustration and commits it to God's hands, confident that He will use it and fulfill it.

Suggested Closing Hymns "What Wondrous Love Is This"; "Were You There When They Crucified My Lord?"

Benediction

". . . To him who loves us and has freed us from our sins by his blood and made us a kingdom, priests to his God and Father, to him be glory and dominion for ever and ever. *Amen*" (Revelation 1:5, 6).

EASTER

TRADITIONAL SERVICE

Call to Worship

O the depth of the riches and wisdom and knowledge of God! How unsearchable are his judgments and how inscrutable his ways! . . . For from him and through him and to him are all things. To him be glory forever (Romans 11:33, 36).

Invocation

O Thou who makest the stars and turnest the shadow of death into the morning: On this day of days we meet to render to Thee, our Lord and King, the tribute of our praise; for the resurrection of the springtime, for the everlasting hopes that rise within the human heart, and for the gospel which hath brought life and immortality to light. Receive our thanksgiving, reveal Thy presence, and send forth into our hearts the Spirit of the risen Christ.

Scripture Lessons

Psalms: 50:1–7, 23; 97:1, 2, 4–12; 111; 115; 116:1–9; 118:1–7, 17.

Old Testament: Isaiah 25:1–9. Ezekiel 37:9–14.

New Testament: Matthew 27:57—28:20. Mark 15:42—16:20. Luke 23:50—24:18. John 19:38—20:18. 1 Corinthians 15:12–20, 53–57. Revelation 1:10–18.

Easter Litany

LEADER From the dust of vainly traveled highways and the weariness of almost forgotten hopes,

RESPONSE Lift up our eyes to Thee, O Lord.

LEADER From the mysteries of evil, and pain, and sorrow, and from the dark records of history and tradition,

RESPONSE Lift up our eyes to Thee, O Lord.

LEADER From the depths of sin, the limitations of our vision, the failures of our will, the littleness of our spiritual experience,

RESPONSE Lift up our eyes to Thee, O Lord.

LEADER That we may know life with its eternal setting and become new creatures with minds set on things above,

RESPONSE Grant us the victory, we pray.

LEADER That we may transform every defeat into triumph, every opposition into a way of help, and every sacrifice into a new attainment,

RESPONSE Grant us the victory, we pray.[27]

Pastor's Easter Prayer

Righteous and ever-living God, whose Son on this day didst shatter the power of death, bringing life and immortality to light: We worship Thee. On this day of all days in humanity's history, assist us that we fail not in low aim or dull sensitiveness to its high significance. Intensify our feelings that already are athrob with emotions stirred by Thee and the eternal suggestions of this day. Give us the joy of the Resurrection that turned night into light and mourning into laughter, to lighten up our too frequently drab lives. Give us the power of the Resurrection, which broke the reign of death, to shatter every ancient tyranny that entombs Thy people: The intrigues of war, the subtlety of highly vested interests, contemptuous racial pride, and ambitious self-seekers. Give us the victory of Easter that turned a cross into a Resurrection, and made the one-time symbol of shame the sign of Thy conquering hosts, to capture spiritual triumph from our worst material defeats, to make sickness a refining ministry to character, to transform tragedy into faith, and all bitterness into love. Give us the peace of the Resurrection that calmed the terrorized hearts of Thy children of old. Until the day dawns grant us brave hearts and constant spirits; and ever to Thee be praise and glory, world without end. *Amen.*

CONTEMPORARY SERVICE

THE RISEN LORD APPEARS

The Prelude   *Gloria* (Mozart)

The Choral Call

Call to Worship

MINISTER   "This is the day which the Lord has made; let us rejoice and be glad in it" (Psalms 118:24).

PEOPLE   "Christ being raised from the dead, dies no more; death has no more dominion over Him. The whole world's darkness is scattered." (*See* Romans 6:9.)

MINISTER   Rejoice in the Lord always, again I say, *Rejoice!* Let the angelic choirs of heaven now rejoice. Let the divine mysteries rejoice. Let all the earth rejoice. Let the Church rejoice. Let every person here rejoice.

The Hymn of Joy   "Christ the Lord is Risen Today"

Lighting of the Candles Symbolizing Christ Alive

THE RISEN LORD APPEARS
TO ONE IN SORROW

The Scripture Story   John 20:1, 11–18

The Prayer

Eternal God, our Father, we praise Thee for the joy that comes into our hearts on this Easter morn. As the risen Christ brought hope to ones in sorrow long ago, we thank Thee that He can also bring new hope to us. Lift us from the depths of sorrow and sadness, we pray, as we are ever mindful of His victory over death. As Thou hast turned the shadows of death into rays of morning light, wilt Thou illumine our spirits with hope of life eternal, through Jesus Christ our Lord.

Choral Amen

THE RISEN LORD APPEARS
TO ONE WHO DOUBTED

The Scripture Story   John 20:19–29

The Affirmation of Faith

LEADER   As our spirits have weakened under the pressures of temptation and doubt, let us remind ourselves of the great beliefs of our faith.

LEADER AND PEOPLE   We believe in the one God, Maker and Ruler of all things. Father of all men; the Source of all goodness and beauty, all truth and love.

We believe in Jesus Christ, God manifest in the flesh, our Teacher, Example, and Redeemer, the Savior of the world.

We believe in the Holy Spirit, God present with us for guidance, for comfort, and for strength.

We believe in the forgiveness of sins, in the life of love and prayer, and in grace equal to every need.

We believe in the Word of God contained in the Old and New Testaments, as the sufficient rule both of faith and of practice.

We believe in the Church as the fellowship for worship and for service of all who are united to the living Lord.

We believe in the Kingdom of God as the divine rule in human society; and in the brotherhood of man under the Fatherhood of God.

We believe in the final triumph of righteousness, and in the life everlasting. *Amen.*

THE RISEN LORD APPEARS TO THOSE WHO WERE DEFEATED

The Scripture Story   Luke 24:13–32

Hymn   "Look, Ye Saints! The Sight Is Glorious"

THE RISEN LORD APPEARS TO ONE WHO DENIED HIM

The Scripture Story   John 21:1, 4, 9, 15–19

Gloria Patri

The Presentation of Tithes and Offerings

Easter Anthem   "I Know That My Redeemer Liveth"

Doxology and the Prayer of Dedication

THE RISEN LORD APPEARS TO US IN THE SPIRIT

The Easter Sermon   "Turning Scars Into Stars"

The Hymn of Triumph   "Crown Him With Many Crowns"

Benediction

"Now may the God of peace who brought again from the dead our Lord Jesus, the great shepherd of the sheep, by the blood of the eternal covenant, equip you with everything good that you may do his will, working in you that which is pleasing in his sight, through Jesus Christ; to whom be glory for ever and ever. *Amen*" (Hebrews 13:20, 21).

Postlude   "Trumpet Triumphant in C" (Purcell) or "Lenten Postlude" (Kock)

Section 7

CHRISTMAS SERVICES

Celebration of the Birth of Our Lord

Traditional Service

*Contemporary Christmas Service
of Carols and Candles*

Meditation: "Christmas Is . . ."

Hanging of the Greens

CELEBRATION OF THE BIRTH OF OUR LORD

To put Christ into the contemporary Christmas celebration is the responsibility of the Church and the Christian home.

It is trite yet nonetheless true that secularism has taken over much of today's observance. Not all of that is bad when it demonstrates goodwill, generosity, family togetherness, and help to the needy.

However, it is incumbent upon the church to provide advent preparation for celebrating the great Christ-event, and to do it meaningfully and appealingly.

Christmas affords the opportunity to honor the gift of God's love as demonstrated in one of the most decisive events in history. Christian families likewise can plan this dimension into their own holiday schedule of activities. To these high purposes, this material is designed to aid.

TRADITIONAL SERVICE

Call to Worship

Glory to God in the highest, and on earth peace among men with whom he is pleased! (Luke 2:14).

Invocation

O God of Love, who centuries ago blessed our earth in the form of Jesus Christ: With glad hearts we come to adore Thee, to rekindle our sense of wonder in Thy majestic ways, and to look to the Christ as our Star of Hope. Forbid that we should be preoccupied with lesser interests and transient pleasures, that no room is left for Him who is the King of kings and the Prince of peace, even Jesus the Saviour of the world. *Amen.*

Scripture Lessons

Psalms: 89:1–7, 19–22, 24; 98; 103; 148.

Old Testament: Isaiah 2:2–5; 9:2–7.

New Testament: Matthew 1:18–25; 2:1–23. John 1:1–34. Titus 2:11; 3:15. Hebrews 1.

Christmas Litany

LEADER   For the life of Jesus Christ, through whom Thou hast revealed Thy love to us,

RESPONSE   We praise Thy name, O God.

LEADER   For our share in the selfishness which rules our every day, the prejudices and suspicions which divide men, the love of unworthy things which cheapens life, and the indifference which allows evils contrary to Thy revealed will to go unchecked,

RESPONSE   Forgive us, Dear Lord.

LEADER   May a new birth of Christ's Spirit come into our hearts that our minds might be purified, our affections kindled, our compassion for the suffering quickened, our service made more generous, and our zeal for righteousness and peace more intense,

RESPONSE   We implore Thee, through Jesus Christ our Lord. *Amen.*

Pastor's Christmas Prayer

God of Grace and God of Glory: Before Thy throne we humble ourselves, seeking forgiveness for our feeble efforts to understand the magnitude and meaning of Christ's birth and for our indifference to that for which He lived and died. For the trifling selfishness that fills our time with other things, our mind with other thoughts, our hearts with other loves, and the rooms of our lives with lesser guests until Christ is crowded out, we plead Thy forgiveness, O God. At this Christmas season, give us the disposition to let Christ be born anew within each of our lives, creating in us a new outlook, new serenity, firmer convictions, and a new spirit.

May the Spirit of Jesus help heal the wounds and scars left by misunderstanding, betrayal of trust, and evil deeds. Help those who have been wronged to forgive and those who have wronged to repent. Cleanse us of ambitions that have no rightful place in the Christian heart. Turn our eyes to men and women whose hopes have turned to ashes; our ears to the cries of children denied proper chances in life; and our energies to those caught in complex circumstances.

We pray for love and goodness to those who have no Christmas—for boys and girls whose hands press against store windows while their eyes devour the glories they can never touch. We pray penitence for those who think they are having Christmas, but have none because of hearts torn by hate, twisted by prejudice, crippled by pride, and betrayed by deceit. We pray for stepping-stones to higher things for children in whose homes the candles have been put out by fear and pestilence, and for the darkened millions who go to bed hungry. We pray for faith, patience, and consolation to those whose homes are empty with the passing of loved ones. Tie these cares to our hearts, O God. *Amen.*

CONTEMPORARY SERVICE
OF CAROLS AND CANDLES

Preparation for Worship (*Instrumental music: violin, harp, trumpet, and so forth*)

Choral Call to Worship

Opening Hymn "Joy to the World"

Call to Worship
"The angel said, 'Behold, I bring you good tidings of great joy, which shall be to all people. For unto you is born this day in the city of David, a Saviour, which is Christ the Lord.' " . . . "Thanks be unto God for his unspeakable gift" (Luke 2:10; 2 Corinthians 9:15 KJV).

Invocation
Our God and Father, we come to Thee rejoicing in the gift of Thy Son to the world. We turn our thoughts toward the

birth of Jesus Christ who brought light into the world. Bless us, as in our worship we travel again to Bethlehem and pray as Jesus taught us:

Unison Lord's Prayer

Choral Response

THE PROMISE OF THE LIGHT OF THE WORLD

His Coming Foretold   Isaiah 9:2–7

A Carol   "It Came Upon the Midnight Clear"

THE PREPARATION FOR HIS COMING

The Annunciation   Luke 1:26–33

A Carol   "What Child Is This?"

The Offering

Anthem   "Let Our Gladness Have No End" (Neske); or "Holy Night" (Adam)

Carol   "We Three Kings" (*as offering is brought to chancel*)

Dedication Prayer for Christmas Offering:
   O Lord of light and life, as of old, men came from watching in their fields, and kings from their dominions to behold the Savior born in a manger; so we come from our various fields of work to worship Thee. Bless these gifts that we bring, so that the light of hope and peace may shine in power over the entire world, through Jesus Christ. *Amen.*

THE COMING OF THE CHRIST CHILD

The Fulfillment of the Promise   Luke 2:1–17

Solo   "The Birthday of the King"

The Christmas Sermon   "God's Unspeakable Gift"

Carol   "O Little Town of Bethlehem"

THE SERVICE OF LIGHTS

Communion Prayer

FOR THE BREAD   We praise thee, O God, and bless Thy holy
name, because Thou hast not withheld Thy mercy from our
sinful race; but in the fullness of time humbled Thyself in
the Incarnation and gave Thyself in the Crucifixion that we
might receive adoption and eternal salvation. Bless this sacred bread that we eat so that Jesus Christ may invade our
being, for Thy name's sake. *Amen.*

FOR THE CUP   O God, we bow in adoration for the Christ
Child, who grew up to become a Man of spotless humanity,
tender charity, spiritual power, amazing love, and faithfulness unto death. Grant us to receive of His fullness and
grace, so that we might experience the turning on of light
within, which comes from the Spirit of the indwelling Christ.
Then so perfect us in His likeness, that we may be lights in
the dark world and experience at last His triumph and glory
in heaven. *Amen.*

Choir   "One Little Candle" (Roach and Mysels)

Communion Participation

Please come forward to serve yourself; then take a candle,
light it, and form a large circle around the sanctuary.

Carol   "Silent Night"

Christmas Blessing

Blessed are you who find Christmas in the age-old story of a
babe born in Bethlehem.

To you a little child will always mean hope and promise
to a troubled world.

Blessed are you who find Christmas in the joy of gifts sent
lovingly to others.

You shall share the gladness and joy of the shepherds and
wise men of old.

Blessed are you who find Christmas in the fragrant greens,
the cheerful holly, and soft flicker of candles.

To you shall come bright memories of love and happiness.

Blessed are you who find Christmas in the Christmas star.

Your lives may ever reflect its beauty and light.

Blessed are you who find Christmas in the happy music of Christmastime.

You shall have a song of joy ever singing in your heart.

Blessed are you who find Christmas in the message of the Prince of Peace.

You will ever strive to help Him bring peace on earth, goodwill to men.[28]

Benediction

While you are placed among the things that are passing away into darkness, may you ever cling to those that shall abide in Jesus Christ. Let your light shine before men to illumine the darkness. God bless you everyone. *Amen.*

Postlude   "Christmas Morn" (Handel)

MEDITATION: CHRISTMAS IS . . .

Christmas is believing in the spirit of Santa Claus even when you know that no such person really exists . . .

Christmas is licking stamps and sealing envelopes until one's tongue tastes like a glue factory . . .

Christmas is crawling out of the self-centeredness of an old miserly Scrooge and giving to make someone happy . . .

Christmas is a small child with nose pressed flat against a store window with an undying hope in his heart . . .

Christmas is kissing under the mistletoe someone you truly love—or think you love . . .

Christmas is a small child singing a lullaby to her new doll with the sentiment of a Raphael Madonna . . .

Christmas is shopping for gifts for loved ones and friends and spending more than one can really afford . . .

Christmas is the wonder and awe in the eyes of a child, as she tenderly places and replaces the figures of the nativity scene . . .

Christmas is the warm, cordial feeling one has for family and friends while baking Christmas goodies . . .

Christmas is being awakened early Christmas morning by a small child who asks excitedly, "Has Santa been here yet?"

Christmas is a boy spending money for a special gift to his first girl friend . . .

Christmas is the magic and beauty of multicolored lights—crystal snowflakes—the voices singing harmonious carols that break the silence of the night . . .

Christmas is sharing our abundance with children who have no chance and the aged who have grown weary . . .

Christmas is the sound of coins being dropped in the Salvation Army kettle . . .

Christmas is the simple faith and mysterious awe one feels as the family sits before the fire reading the Christmas story from the Bible . . .

Christmas is the strange claim that God should enter into man's affairs thru a baby born of peasants in a humble stable in a far away land: Thus to give a new lease on life . . .

Christmas is the Christ spirit in one person finding the kinship with the Christ spirit in another person . . .

Christmas is saying with Tiny Tim: "Merry Christmas and God bless us every one!"

MARGARET CHRISTENSEN

HANGING OF THE GREENS[29]

Explanation *This service is planned for decorating the sanctuary prior to Christmas in the midst of worship. Sunday-school classes are used, with a family representative hanging a decorating piece. The major decorating should be done in advance, with only a specified number of pieces added equaling the number of* *classes. During the course of the service, representatives of each class leave their places to hang the greens. Either the various graded choirs or Sunday-school departments sing. Adults and youth read the Scriptures. Following the service, a tasting party is held where all classes or women's groups have provided Christmas goodies. This service takes immense organization; however, herein is the secret of its beauty, meaning, and participation.*

Musical Introduction

ORCHESTRA   Medley of Christmas Music

CARILLON MUSIC   "Let All Mortal Flesh Keep Silence"

ORGAN PRELUDE   "Silent Night" (*During this number the candles are lit.*)

PROCESSIONAL HYMN   "O Come, All Ye Faithful"

Call to Worship and Invocation

THE PROPHECY   Isaiah 9:2–7

Hanging of the Greens   (*Families from classes hang decorations.*)

ANTHEM   "Break Forth O Beauteous Heavenly Light"—Bach

THE ANNUNCIATION   Luke 1:26–33

Hanging of the Greens   (*Families from classes hang decorations.*)

CAROL   "Angels We Have Heard on High"—Youth Choir (*Congregation joins in singing first verse.*)

THE MAGNIFICAT   Luke 1:45–55

Hanging of the Greens   (*Families from classes hang decorations.*)

CAROL   "Deck the Halls"—Junior Choir

THE FULFILLMENT   Luke 2:1–20

Hanging of the Greens   (*Families from classes hang decorations.*)

CAROL   "Little Baby Jesus"—Cherub Choir

The Evening Prayer   Eternal God, who has declared love to all men through the birth and life of Jesus Christ, our hearts are filled with gratitude for all that this season brings. We are mindful of the stars that shed light upon the earth and bear us back in memory to Bethlehem, and the carols that fill the air retelling the story of a humble manger where our Saviour was born. May these decorations of wreaths, bells, ribbons, and banners, which we have hung tonight for eyes to see, give glory to the Prince of Peace. Grant, O Father, that His love of peace, His faith in things unseen, His pity for the poor, His actions of love, His vision of the coming age shall find room in the inn of our hearts. So may we live at peace with one another and with all Your family, through the Spirit of Jesus Christ the Lord. *Amen.*

Hanging of the Greens (*Families from classes hang decorations.*)
CAROL "What Child Is This?"—Children's Choir
ANTHEM "*Gloria in Excelsis*"—Sanctuary Choir

Meditation "Behind Our Christmas Traditions" The true Christmas story centers in the Christ Child, but it began long before that. It is a story that has changed with the passing of history and the transforming power of human experiences. Each generation of mankind adds to and subtracts from the pattern of the story. Let us see why we now follow certain traditions and customs when we celebrate Christmas today.

Our story goes back to at least four thousand years ago and possibly longer than that. It begins in Mesopotamia, called the cradle of civilization. Here Christmas really began as the festival which renewed the world for another year. Here began the "twelve days" of Christmas, the festivals, the bright fires, the giving of gifts, the carnivals, merrymakings, and clownings, the mummers who sang and played from house to house, the church processions with their lights and songs. All these and more began centuries before Christ was born. And they celebrated the arrival of a New Year.

All peoples all over the world learned from Mesopotamia. Everything happening there was in the course of time imitated by its neighbors—imitated, yet never copied exactly. Thus it changed its face as it went. One road traveled through Greece to Rome and another road led from Asia Minor through the Balkans, up the Danube Valley into the heart of Europe.

The Northland peoples knew that winter followed summer, and that spring followed winter, and that winter was the time when all nature's green life died except in the evergreens. All the Northland cherished the evergreen that did not die. Thus long before the Christian era, evergreens were used as an emblem of eternal life.

Holly was symbolic of joy and peace, and primitive people would hang it over their doors in the form of wreaths to entice spirits to bring good luck. Why a circle? Because a circle is the symbol of timelessness, and the green leaves of life everlasting.

According to some sources, Christ's crown of thorns had been fashioned from holly leaves. At first its berries were white, but when the crown was pressed down on His brow, blood drops turned the berries a bright red.

Because holly was originally regarded as magic, it was believed that if a house were hung at Christmas with thorny holly, the husband would rule throughout the year; if hung with smooth holly, the woman would be master.

Since mistletoe grows as a parasite at the top of trees, it was symbolic of the link between heaven and earth to the ancient people. The Druids believed that it contained a sacred spirit. Priests dressed in long flowing robes marched into the forest followed by men, women, and children. Trumpets were sounded and bards chanted as they approached the sacred oak trees upon which the mistletoe grew. The high priest carried a gold curved knife with which he cut down the mistletoe. He threw it down to young beautiful girls who caught the sprigs in a sparkling white cloth. The mistletoe was not allowed to touch the earth or it would bring bad luck. The priest then gave to everyone a sprig to hang over their doors at home, and all who entered received a "kiss of peace."

Among the Romans, the mistletoe was also considered a symbol of hope and peace. Therefore, when enemies met under it, they laid aside their weapons, kissed each other, and declared a truce until the next day.

Where did we get our Christmas tree and when did it arrive? Giving reverence to green trees in the dead of winter and decorating them goes so far back into antiquity that we cannot trace the origin. The early Egyptians took green date palms into their homes significant of "life triumphant over death," and when the ancient pagans of the Northland were converted to Christianity, the evergreen tree came to denote His bringing new life to the world after the long days of winter.

Martin Luther is credited with putting lights on the Christmas tree. The story goes that he was walking home through a forest one night. He was so impressed by the beautiful stars in the winter sky and by the stately evergreens that he tried to explain all the glory to his family when he arrived home. Words failed him, so he went out and cut a small fir tree and placed lighted candles on it to represent the starry sky above the stable the night that Christ was born.

Did you know that there was once a real Santa Claus? He was born St. Nicholas late in the third century of Christian parents, and died December 6 in the fourth century. When he was a very young man, he decided to devote his life to Christian service. He was such a remarkable person that many varied and numerous legends have been gathered about his life on earth, and his life as a saint after his death. Although his job in America comes but once a year, his work in Europe and Asia lasts all year round. In fact, he is probably the hardest working saint of all. All over the world, sailors and travelers, and even countries revere and honor him, and he is a patron saint. Most countries celebrate his memory December 6 with exchange of gifts.

One of Nicholas's chief characteristics was his unsurpassed generosity. He soon learned how many people were oppressed with poverty, and he often went out in disguise and distributed presents, especially to children. Thus he became the patron saint of children everywhere. His fame spread far and wide all over the world, and so today it is good that the memory of generous St. Nicholas is still alive, for he brings happiness to millions of children.

The true Christmas story centers in the birth of Christ depicted by the nativity scene. This is a Christmas custom that Saint Francis of Assisi made popular.

During the Middle Ages there were very few books, and even if there had been more, people could not read them. Church ceremonies were conducted in Latin, so that Christmas had little meaning for many who attended. This worried St. Francis, for he wanted to humanize the teaching of the Scriptures and to show his followers that Christ also came from humble beginnings. So he assembled the necessary properties—a manger, star, a live ox, and a donkey. Real persons took the parts of Mary, Joseph, and the shepherds. St. Francis arranged the scene and placed a life-size wax figure of the Christ Child in the manger. For the first time many understood the true meaning of the Christmas story. As they stood before the manger, the good saint led his people in songs of praises to the Christ Child and from his "jovial singing" came a new idea about the holiday season—the singing of Christmas carols. Everyone was so impressed by the Christmas ceremony and the singing of the carols that the rites were repeated year after year and soon the custom spread through the world.

Only a few of the customs and traditions that we observe today have been mentioned here. All these and many more have come to us from our historic past. In this moment of time in which we are living, we are a part of that past, the past which brings to us the finest traditions of men and women who have given to Christmas their deepest and enduring selves. Christmas is an expression of a faith and hope which for generations have answered death with a song of triumph. After thousands of years the festival that has grown about the birth of the Christ Child remains an affirmation that all things can be made anew.

CAROL   "Joy to the World"—All

Benediction   (CONGREGATION *remains seated.*)

CAROL OF DISMISSAL   "Lord, Dismiss Us With Thy Blessing"
   (*medley of carols as congregation is ushered out one row at a
   time, starting from the rear—tasting party follows*)

Section 8

SPECIAL CHURCH SERVICES

Baby Blessing and Parent Dedication

Church Building Dedication

Installation of Church Officers

Installation of a Minister

IN THE LOCAL CHURCH

BABY BLESSING AND
PARENT DEDICATION

Explanation

_____, you have brought this child, _____, into this sacred place of worship for God's anointment and your dedication of yourselves to rear the child in the Christian way of life.

It has scriptural precedent, for Jesus our Lord, as a baby, was brought by Mary and Joseph to the Temple, where the prophet Simeon took Him in his arms, blessed Him according to their custom, and they dedicated themselves to the sacred responsibility.

This is a service of thanksgiving to God for the joy and hope that has come into your lives by the presence of this child. It is recognition of God as the Giver of Life and an affirmation that all children are His. It is a reconsecration of yourselves.

The love of a home will help determine (his) future characteristics. God will enrich (his) life, if you will keep the doors of your own lives open to God.

Do you dedicate your child to God? ANSWER: We do.

Do you promise to give your child the best that you have learned of the ways and love of your Heavenly Father, so that (he) may grow into the love and nurture and admonition of the Lord? ANSWER: We do.

Pastoral Prayer

Heavenly Father, gracious and merciful, we thank Thee that Thou has given these the privilege of parenthood, and has blessed their home with this little life.

183

Bless this child, O Lord, with strength of body, soundness of mind, and health of soul.

Help these parents to keep Christian values, to develop Christian priorities, and to walk in the paths committed to faith, truth, justice, and righteousness so that this child may grow toward Thee. Grant them patience and wisdom, good judgment and balance for this demanding task, in the name of Jesus Christ. (PASTOR *takes* BABY *in arms.*)

This is _____, born _____. The paternal grandparents are _____. The maternal grandparents are _____.

Blessing Prayer

"The Lord bless you and keep you: the Lord make his face to shine upon you, and be gracious to you: the Lord lift up his countenance upon you, and give peace" [throughout your life. *Amen.*] (Numbers 6:24–26).

CHURCH BUILDING DEDICATION

Prelude   MARCHE TRIUMPHOLE (Guilmont)

Call to Worship

"I was glad when they said to me, 'Let us go to the house of the Lord!' " (Psalms 122:1).

Processional Hymn   "God of Our Fathers, Whose Almighty Hand"

Introit

MINISTER   "Give thanks to the Lord, call on his name, make known his deeds among the peoples!"

RESPONSE   "Sing to him, sing praises to him, tell of all his wonderful works!" (Psalms 105:1, 2).

CHORAL RESPONSE   "Rejoice Ye Pure in Heart" (*refrain only*)

MINISTER   "We have thought on thy steadfast love, O God, in the midst of thy temple."

RESPONSE   "As thy name, O God, so thy praise reaches to the ends of the earth" (Psalms 48:9, 10).

CHORAL RESPONSE   (*Same as above*)

MINISTER   Let us pray.

Unison Prayer

O Lord, our God, exalted above all, of whom the stars sing and whose voice is heard within our hearts; receive our adoration and praise, through Jesus Christ. *Amen.*

Hymn of Praise   "All Hail the Power of Jesus' Name" or "The Church's One Foundation"

Reading of the Scriptures   Psalms 84:1-5, 10-12

Messages of Greetings

The Offering

Doxology

Anthem   "All Glory, Laud, and Honor"

Dedicatory Sermon   "The Place Where Thy Glory Dwells"

Ceremony of Dedication

MINISTER   Having been prospered by our God, and enabled by His grace and power to complete this church building to be used for the glory of His name, we now stand in His holy presence, and dedicate this church. (CONGREGATION *please stand.*) Recognizing our own unworthiness and our reliance upon God for wisdom and strength; conscious of the faith, sacrifices, and love expressed that has made this possible; acknowledging those by whose knowledge, artistic thought, and skillful labor this beautiful temple was wrought; remembering all who have loved and served and led this church, especially those who now have joined the Church Triumphant . . .

PEOPLE   We, the congregation of this church, dedicate this building to God, our Father, from whom comes every good and perfect gift; to the honor of Jesus Christ our Lord and Saviour; to the praise of the Holy Spirit, Source of light and life; and to the work of the whole Church.

MINISTER   For the assembling together of the rich and the
poor to praise God who is the Master of them all; for the
worship of Him in spirit and truth; for the preaching of the
Word of God in its fullness; for the administration of the
sacraments proclaiming our Lord Jesus Christ as our Saviour from sin; for contemplation of beauty, and the ex-
periencing of music . . .

PEOPLE   We dedicate this sanctuary to the Lord our God.

MINISTER   For the comfort of those who mourn; for the
strength of those who are tempted; for the sanctification of
the family; for the building of character; for the giving of
hope and courage to all human hearts . . .

PEOPLE   We dedicate this chapel to the Lord our God.

MINISTER   To the joy of bread broken together, as Jesus di-
vided with those who loved Him; to the instruction and
training of children, youth, and adults; for the development
of artistic talents; for the performance of useful service; and
to the art of meditation and communion with the unseen and
eternal . . .

PEOPLE   We dedicate the fellowship hall, the library, the fine-
arts studio, the offices, and the prayer room (*and other*).

MINISTER   As a tribute of gratitude and love, and as an offering of thanksgiving and praise from those who have tasted
the cup of Thy salvation and experienced the riches of Thy
grace . . .

PEOPLE   We, the people of this church and congregation, now
consecrating ourselves anew, dedicate this entire house of
the Lord to the worship of Almighty God, and for service to
our fellowmen, in the Spirit of Jesus Christ our Lord and
Saviour.

Dedication Prayer

Almighty God, our Heavenly Father, by whose will and
blessings we have built this edifice; now we gratefully dedicate
it solely to Thee. We express loving appreciation to Thee for
those faithful stewards who have given sacrificially and willingly to make this dream a reality. We express to Thee our ap-

preciation for those skilled craftsmen who have turned timbers and stone into this sacred temple.

For worship, preaching, teaching, and the ministry of comfort in the name of Jesus Christ, and to Thy majestic glory, we set aside this building.

May the favor of the Lord our God be upon us, now and evermore. *Amen.*

Choral Response   (CHILDREN'S CHOIR)

Dedication Hymn   "God of Grace and God of Glory"

Benediction
May the Lord bless your coming in and your going out, and establish you in every good work and word, both now and forever. *Amen.*

Postlude   "Festival Toccatu" (Fletcher)

INSTALLATION OF CHURCH OFFICERS

A Covenant of Fidelity   (*It may be asked of those being installed.*) Do you each accept the office to which you have been elected (or appointed), and do you promise, the Lord being your helper, faithfully to fulfill its duties?

The Response (*in unison*)   I do.

A Covenant of the Older Officers   (*Officers whose terms have not expired should stand.*) Do you gladly receive these as fellow officers serving with you in their varied responsibilities, covenanting to work together as laborers with God? If so, please indicate your willingness by saying in unison, I do.

The Response (*in unison*)   I do.

A Covenant by the Congregation (*or Group*)   Will you pledge your eager support to the work of God in this congregation (or organization) under the leadership of these, your fellow members who have been selected to serve (or, whom you have elected to office), and will you renew your vows of fidelity by standing and engaging with me in a common covenant?

The Response (*in unison*)   We will.

The Covenant (*in unison*)   Affirming our membership in the holy Church throughout all the world, and our fellowship in this congregation with those who have obtained a like precious faith, we renew our vows of fidelity to our Lord Jesus Christ, and solemnly covenant and promise:

That we will walk together in brotherly love, as is becoming in members of a Christian church; that we will not forsake the assembling of ourselves together; that we will endeavor to bring up such as may at any time be under our care, in the nurture and admonition of the Lord, and by a pure and holy example, to win our kindred and acquaintances to the Saviour, to holiness, and to eternal life; that we will regularly support the work of the church by systematic contributions of money.

The Installation Prayer   Set apart, O Lord, these Thy servants, to the work whereunto they have been called by the voice of the Church. Endue them plenteously with heavenly wisdom. Grant them Thy grace, that they may be good men (and/or women) full of the Holy Spirit and of faith, ruling in the fear of God. Give them that favor and influence with the people which come from following Christ. So fill them with His Spirit that they may lead this congregation (or people) in His service. Make them faithful unto death, and when the Chief Shepherd shall appear, may they receive a crown of glory that fadeth not away. *Amen.*

INSTALLATION OF A SENIOR OR ASSOCIATE MINISTER

Prelude Music

Call to Worship
LEADER   "Praise the Lord."
PEOPLE   "I will give thanks to the Lord with my whole heart,

in the company of the upright, in the congregation" (Psalms 111:1, 2).

LEADER   "Great is the Lord and greatly to be praised in the city of our God!"

PEOPLE   "His holy mountain, beautiful in elevation, is the joy of all the earth, Mount Zion ... the city of the great King" (48:1, 2).

Hymn "Glorious Things of Thee Are Spoken"

Invocation

Eternal God, whose purpose in Creation was revealed in Jesus Christ, who through the centuries has called men to give themselves to establish Thy will on earth and the church to be the redeeming community; bless with Thy Spirit the relationship of church and minister which has been established through Jesus Christ, who taught us to pray:

Unison Lord's Prayer and Choral Response

Statement of Purpose

Today this church celebrates an important and decisive milestone in its history. We are gathered to formally install _____ as the minister (*or associate minister*) of _____.

Installation Service for Minister

The chairperson of the church (board) will now bring _____ and (his) family to the chancel.

The Scripture Readings

Old Testament   Isaiah 61:1–3.
New Testament   Romans 10:9–15; Matthew 28:18–20.

Hymn "I Love Thy Kingdom, Lord" or "I Love to Tell the Story"

Sermon "The Mutual Obligations in Ministry"

Anthem "How Beautiful Upon the Mountains" (Harper)

Presentation of the New Minister

CHAIRPERSON OF THE CHURCH (*board*) The church (board), upon recommendation of the personnel committee, has approved the calling of our (brother), _____, to the position of _____. (He) has moved to our city with his family, whom I now wish to introduce to you.
(*Introduction of the individuals of the family.*)
The credentials will be presented by the chairperson of the personnel committee.

Minister's Credentials Read

CHAIRPERSON OF PERSONNEL COMMITTEE (*Here should be presented the family data, educational background, pastoral experience, and notable accomplishments.*)

Ceremony of Installation

CHAIRPERSON OF (ELDERS) Inasmuch as this sacred act involves mutual obligations, as the chairperson of the (elders) I will call upon you to unite in a covenant of installation. _____, will you stand?

Do you accept the responsibilities of the office to which you have been called, and do you reaffirm your ordination vows, and promise to give yourself wholly to your ministry, to exemplify the life of your Master, and to conduct yourself in such a manner as to reflect credit to Christ and His Church?

MINISTER TO BE INSTALLED Willingly I reaffirm my ordination vows; believing with all my heart that Jesus is the Christ, the Son of the Living God, and accepting the Holy Scriptures as inspired of God through the Holy Spirit, it is my desire to devote my life to the ministry of the Word; so to live as to bring credit and not dishonor to the Gospel which I preach, and to fulfill to my utmost ability the office of a good minister of Jesus Christ. I will diligently and faithfully perform all of my duties on behalf of the congregation. (*Minister may be seated.*)

CHAIRPERSON OF THE BOARD Will the members of the church (board) please stand and make their commitment.

(BOARD) MEMBERS (*in unison*) We covenant with God and with our new minister to be loyal to this church and to its head, Jesus Christ, by our consistent attendance, willing service, cooperative spirit, supportive conversation, sacrificial stewardship, and abiding friendship.

CHAIRPERSON OF CONGREGATION Will the congregation please stand and make your declaration?

MEMBERS (*in unison*) Affirming our membership in Christ's Church, and our fellowship in this congregation with those of like faith, we renew our vows of fidelity to our Lord Jesus Christ, and our allegiance to His Church, solemnly covenanting to work together with our minister to extend the Gospel in its purity and power in this community and throughout the world, and, as faithful servants of the Lord, to give our minister our utmost support in every way, according to our abilities and opportunities.[30]

CHAIRPERSON OF CONGREGATION   Let all remain standing.

Prayer of Installation

Our Father, we pray Thy blessing upon this new minister as (he) assumes the sacred duties with which (he) has been entrusted. Make (his) ministry to be the means of awakening the careless, of strengthening the faithful, of comforting the afflicted, and of edifying the church. Guard (him) against temptation; keep (his) heart pure and steadfast.

Grant to (him) Thy Spirit; Thy love that (he) may win men to Christ; Thy forgiveness that (he) may teach forgiveness; Thy sacrificial Spirit that (he) may go where Thy will directs.

O Lord, bless this congregation, that they may be receptive to leadership and faithful in support. Prepare their minds to receive Thy Word; their hearts to receive Thy love; their wills to receive Thy commission. Sustain them in the bonds of unity; establish them in righteousness; and develop them into Thy community of love; through Jesus Christ, our Lord.

Hymn   "God of Grace and God of Glory"

Benediction

"Let the favor of the Lord our God be upon us, and establish thou the work of our hands . . . yea, the work of our hands establish thou it" (Psalms 90:17). Let Thy loving-kindness, O Lord, be upon us.

Section 9

PATRIOTIC SERVICES

Freedom and Democracy Sunday

Memorial Day

Independence Day

Section 9

PATRIOTIC SERVICES

Freedom and Democracy Sunday

Memorial Day

GOD AND COUNTRY

FREEDOM AND DEMOCRACY SUNDAY
(or Other Suitable Occasion)

Prelude

INSTRUMENTALISTS (*processional hymn*) "God of Our Fathers" (*traditional, with trumpets and timpani; two Boy or Girl Scouts present the colors: the American and Christian flags*)

ALL (*American flag salute, unison*)

ALL (*Christian flag salute, unison*) I pledge allegiance to the Christian flag and to the Saviour for whose Kingdom it stands—one brotherhood, uniting all mankind in service and in love.

LEADER (*invocation*) Kind Providence: We are glad we live in America where we are free to choose our occupations, our leaders, our life-style; to speak our mind and to live according to our own religious scruples. We acknowledge the paradox, however, that only in servitude to Jesus Christ are we truly free. So commit us to use our freedom to be our best and not our worst in the Spirit of Jesus Christ. *Amen.*

LEADER The birthright of every American is freedom. As the Preamble to the Constitution reads:

We the people of the United States, in order to form a more perfect Union, establish justice, insure domestic tranquility, provide for the common defense, promote the general welfare, and secure the blessings of liberty to ourselves and our posterity, do ordain and establish this Constitution for the United States of America.

ALL (*contemporary hymn*) "Born Free"

SPEAKING CHORUS Choral—"I Am the Nation" by Otto Whittaker (*lights dim with spot on flag*)

I was born on July 4, 1776, and the Declaration of Independence is my birth certificate. The bloodlines of the world run in my veins, because I offered freedom to the oppressed. I am many things, and many people. I AM THE NATION.

I am 200 million living souls—and the ghost of millions who have lived and died for me.

I am Nathan Hale and Paul Revere. I stood at Lexington and fired the shot heard around the world. I am Washington, Jefferson, and Patrick Henry. I am John Paul Jones, the Green Mountain boys, and Davy Crockett. I am Lee, Grant, and Abe Lincoln.

I remember the Alamo, the *Maine,* and Pearl Harbor. When freedom called, I answered and stayed until it was over, over there. I left my heroic dead in Flanders Fields, on the rock of Corregidor, on the bleak slopes of Korea, and in the steaming jungle of Vietnam.

I am the Brooklyn Bridge, the wheat lands of Kansas, and the granite hills of Vermont. I am the coal fields of the Virginias and Pennsylvania, the fertile lands of the West, the Golden Gate and the Grand Canyon. I am Independence Hall, the *Monitor* and the *Merrimac.*

I am big. I sprawl from the Atlantic to the Pacific ... my arms reach out to embrace Alaska and Hawaii ... three million square miles throbbing with industry. I am more than three million farms. I am forest, field, mountain and desert. I am quiet villages in the country—and teeming cities that never sleep.

You can look at me and see Ben Franklin walking down the streets of Philadelphia with his breadloaf under his arm. You can see Betsy Ross with her needle. You can see the lights of Christmas, and hear the strains of "Auld Lang Syne" as the calendar turns.

I am Babe Ruth and the World Series. I am 130,000 schools and colleges, and 326,000 churches where my people worship God as they think best. I am a ballot dropped in a box, the roar of a crowd in a stadium, and the voice of a choir in a cathedral. I am an editorial in a newspaper and a letter to a congressman.

I am Eli Whitney and Stephen Foster. I am Tom Edison, Albert Einstein, and Billy Graham. I am Horace Greeley, Will Rogers, and the Wright Brothers. I am George Washington Carver, Daniel Webster, and Jonas Salk.

I am Longfellow, Harriet Beecher Stowe, Walt Whitman, and Thomas Paine.

Yes, I am the nation, and these are the things that I am. I was conceived in freedom and, God willing, in freedom will I spend the rest of my days.

May I possess always the integrity, the courage and the strength to keep myself unshackled, to remain a citadel of freedom and a beacon of hope to the world.

I AM THE UNITED STATES.

ALL (*anthem*)   "Give Me Your Tired, Your Poor...."

LEADER   And what is the future of our nation? It has been torn with racial tension, injustice, demonstrations—perhaps these are purposeful in making us a better people—a nation for all people.

As dark and foreboding as it appears, yet there are rays on the horizon.

Thomas Wolfe articulates our faith in saying, "I think the true discovery of America is before us. I think the true fulfillment of our spirit, of our people, of our mighty and immortal land, is yet to come. I think the true discovery of our own democracy is still before us. And I think that all these things are certain as the morning, as inevitable as noon. I think I speak for most men living when I say that our America is Here, is Now, and beckons on before us, and that this glorious assurance is not only our living hope, but our dream to be accomplished."

ALL (*closing hymn*)   "Battle Hymn of the Republic"

LEADER (*benediction*)   Go now, remembering that you are free—by God's good favor. May you be responsible and obedient wherever you are—and the peace and joy of God be with you. *Amen.*

MEMORIAL DAY

Call to Worship

The righteous live for ever, and in the Lord is their reward and the care of them with the most High. Therefore shall they receive the crown of royal dignity and the diadem of beauty from the Lord's hand (The Wisdom of Solomon 5:15–16).

Invocation

Eternal God, Father of our spirits: We rejoice in all who have faithfully lived and triumphantly died. We give Thee thanks for all blessed memories and all enduring hopes; for the ties that bind us to the unseen world; for all the heroic dead who encompass us like a cloud of witnesses. We pray that we who have entered into the heritage of their heroism and self-sacrifice may so honor their memory and so preserve and further their high purposes, that the nation which they defended may stand in all coming years for righteousness and peace, through Jesus Christ, their Lord and ours. *Amen.*[31]

Scripture Lessons

Psalms: 44:1–4, 6, 7, 20–26; 46; 77:1–20; 137:1–6; 145:10–21.
Old Testament: Isaiah 52:3–12.

New Testament: John 14:1–15. 2 Timothy 1:1—2:12. Hebrews 11:17—12:2. 1 Peter 1. Revelation 7:9–17; 21:1–7; 21:23—22:5.

Memorial Litany

LEADER   For the land of our birth, with all its chartered liberties, for all the wonder of our country's story.

RESPONSE   We praise Thee, O God.

LEADER   For leaders in nation and state, and those who in days past and in these present times have labored for the commonwealth; for those who in all times and places have been true and brave, and in the world's common ways have lived upright lives and ministered to their fellows; for those who served their country in her hour of need, and especially for those who gave even their lives,

RESPONSE   We praise Thee, O God.

UNISON   O Almighty God and merciful Father, whose nature
and whose name is Love: As we give Thee thanks for the
courage and the strength vouchsafed to these Thy servants,
we would remember before Thee those who mourn them as
their kindred. Look in mercy upon them; and as this day
brings them memories of those whom they have lost, may it
also bring them consolation from Thee, quickening in them
the sense of communion with the world unseen, and confirming their assurance of that day when Thou shalt restore
to them their own in the very presence of our Lord and Saviour Jesus Christ. *Amen.*

Pastor's Memorial Day Prayer

God of our fathers, who hast made us the heirs of faithful
men of all generations who have given themselves to great
endeavors and made life nobler because they have walked its
ways: We thank Thee for every memory that enriches life
with high ideals and great purposes. We thank Thee for all
who have loved this land which we love, who have been
eager to establish freedom and justice within our borders,
and have given themselves for the fulfillment of their longings. We thank Thee for all who have labored for a friendly
world, free from hatred and bitterness, and have spent
themselves in their pursuit of peace. We thank Thee for all
who in school or laboratory, in church or state, in home or
industry, have sought to fill life with the mind of Christ. We
thank Thee for those dear to us, forgotten by the world but
still living in our hearts, who rest from their labors, and
whose works do follow them. Make this day of memory a
day of peace through our faith that they live with us in Thy
love. Grant that though dead they may still speak to us, bid-
ding us further every cause of righteousness and truth which
they have served, and assuring us that they without us shall
not be made perfect. *Amen.*[32]

INDEPENDENCE DAY

Call to Worship
Blessed is the nation whose God is the Lord, the people whom he has chosen as his heritage (Psalms 33:12).

Invocation
O eternal God, through whose mighty power our fathers won their liberties of old: Grant, we beseech Thee, that we and all the people of this land may have grace to maintain these liberties in righteousness and peace; through Jesus Christ our Lord. *Amen.*[33]

Scripture Lessons
Psalms: 18:1–20; 33:12–22; 48:1–3, 7–14; 107:1–8; 121; 122; 124; 146.

Old Testament: Deuteronomy 4:1–14. Isaiah 26:1–4, 7–8, 12.

New Testament: John 8:31–36. Romans 12:1–13. Galatians 5. 1 Timothy 2; 3. Hebrews 10:32; 11:16; 12:28. 1 Peter 2.

National Litany
LEADER   O God, our Lord, who hast made us one nation out of many peoples: Amid our diversities of race and class and tradition, unite us in a common love of freedom and in high ambitions.

RESPONSE   Help us to establish our land in every righteous way. Maintain our generation in liberty and the struggle for justice and goodwill.

LEADER   O God, remember not the offenses of Thy people; deal not with us after our sins, neither reward us according to our wickedness.

RESPONSE   From the love of ease, blindness of heart, and presumptuous pride, save us, O Lord.

LEADER   From class hatred, racial antagonisms, the seeking of self-advantage and forgetfulness of the general good, save Thy people, O Lord.

UNISON   Teach us, O Lord, to cooperate effectively with other nations, to work for the abolition of war, the establishment of international law, and whatever else may pertain to the general good.

Pastor's Independence Day Prayer

Grant us, O God, a vision of our land, fair as she might be; a land of justice, where none shall prey on others; a land of plenty, where vice and poverty shall cease to fester; a land of brotherhood, where success shall be founded on service, and honor be given to worth alone; a land of peace where order need no longer rest on force, but on the love of all for their land, the great mother of the common life and welfare. Hear Thou, O Lord, the silent prayer of all our hearts, as in city, town, and village we pledge our time and strength and thought to hasten the day of her coming beauty and righteousness; through Jesus Christ our Lord. *Amen.*[34]

Section 10

OUTDOOR OCCASIONS

Campfire Service

Galilean Vesper Service

BY CAMPFIRE OR LAKE

CAMPFIRE SERVICE

Singspiration   (*Someone with guitar leads the singing if possible.*) "Edges of His Ways," "There Must Be a God Somewhere," "Whisper a Prayer," "Kumbaya," "Pass It On," "Spirit of the Living God"

Poem

Twilight in the Foothills

Twilight in the foothills
  Deep'ning into dark.
Far away the nocturne
  Of a meadow lark.

Purple, wooded hill slopes
  Fading out of sight.
Unseen hands are drawing
  The tapestries of night.

Shadowy forms come creeping
  Forth from hidden lairs.
Pines with arms uplifted
  Offer evening prayers.

Soft lights smile a welcome
  To homeward bound,
Where, when tasks are ended,
  Rest and love are found.[35]

Scripture Sentences About Nature

The heavens are telling the glory of God;
  and the firmament proclaims his handiwork.
Psalms 19:1

Thine is the day, thine also the night;
    thou hast established the luminaries and the sun.
Thou hast fixed all the bounds of the earth;
    thou hast made summer and winter.

Psalms 74:16, 17

Prayer of Praise   I am asking you to join me in a prayer that was written nearly seven hundred and fifty years ago by a man in Assisi, Italy, called Francis who knew much about our world. He referred to ants and other creatures, as well as the planets, as "brother," "sister." They are essential fellow-planet riders on whom we depend, and with whom, in God's mysterious grace, this whirling earth is saved from being empty like the moon. As I read the words of Saint Francis, let us pray, with our eyes focused on a star.

Praise be my Lord God with all His creatures and especially our brother the sun, who brings us the day and who brings us light; fair is he and shines with a very great splendor. O Lord, he shows us You.

Praise be my Lord for our sister the moon, and for the stars, which He has set clear and lovely in the heavens.

Praise be my Lord for our brother the wind, and for air and cloud, calms, and all weather by which You uphold life in all creatures.

Praise be my Lord for our sister water, who is very serviceable unto us, and humble and precious and clean.

Praise be my Lord for our brother fire, through whom You give us light in the darkness; and he is bright and pleasant and very strong.

Praise be my Lord for our mother the earth, who sustains us and keeps us and brings forth diverse fruits and flowers of many colors, and grass.

Praise be my Lord for all those who pardon one another for His love's sake, and who endure weakness and tribulation. Blessed are they who peaceably shall endure.

Praise be my Lord for our sister the death of the body, from which no man escapes. Blessed are those who are found walking by Your most holy will.

Praise and bless the Lord; and give thanks to Him; and serve Him with great humility.

SONG "A New Tomorrow"

Scripture (*Choose from* Psalms 139, 8, 121; Job 26:7, 9, 10, 12, 14.)

SOLO "How Great Thou Art"

Thoughts in the Night (*suggested homilies*)
"The Greatness of God" (*homily on Psalm 139*) or
"He Made the Stars Also" (*homily on Genesis 1:16*) or
"God is Speaking (*homily on Psalm 29*)

SILENCE (*while watching the stars*)

Conclusion

ALL "Taps"

> Day is done,
> Gone the sun,
> From the lake,
> From the hill,
> From the sky,
> All is well;
> Safely rest.
> God is nigh.

GALILEAN VESPER SERVICE

Group Singing (*on lake shore*) "Day Is Dying in the West," "Now the Day Is Over," "This Is My Father's World," "Kumbaya"

Sentences of Worship Matthew 6:25-34

Invocation O God, Maker of heaven and earth, and all things visible and invisible; we would commune with You now at eventide, in the cool of the day. May all that is beautiful remind us of You, O Infinite Beauty. May all that is good remind us of You, O Perfect Goodness. May all that is true lead us to You, O Source of all truth. Breathe Your loving Spirit into us all—that we may have eyes to see, ears to hear, and wills to serve in Jesus' name. *Amen.*

Poems

These Things I Like

I like the simple things of earth:
 A daisy on the lawn,
 A violet by the garden gate
 A breath of air at dawn.

I like the lovely things of earth:
 A rainbow in the skies,
 A row of purple irises,
 A pair of shining eyes.

I like the solid things of earth:
 A firm and rugged tree,
 A mammoth boulder on the hill,
 A mighty ship at sea.

I like the lasting things of earth:
 A faith that conquers strife,
 A love that brothers humankind,
 A strong and worthy life.

JOHN C. SLIMP[36]

What Have We Done?

God made the universe.
He made it and called it good.
Clean air, night stars,
Blue sky, green sea splashing,
Animals, birds,
Flowers and grass,
And all things growing.
Man he made—and woman—
In his own image,
Made them for each other.
Good!

A million secrets God hid
For man to discover—
For his use, his growth,
And the joy of his living.

God made it all and called it good,
Gave it to man—and to woman.
"Take it. Use it. Let it serve you,
Meet your needs, be subject to your will,"
He said, smiling.

Man took it—and used it.
He used it up!
Took it for granted!
Took it apart!
And could not put it together.
He smeared the earth, spoiled the sea,
Desecrated the forests
And seemed not to care,
As if not even knowing.

Bottles and cans,
Papers and trash,
Oil slicks, and exhaust fumes,
Polluting—always polluting.
Bombs for war—bombs for peace.
Crashes! Ashes! Always destroying.
Did beauty and duty
Go out together and no one crying?
In his image we were made.
On his good earth he gave us a home.
O God! What have we done?
What have we done?

SAMUEL F. PUGH[37]

Silent Reflection

SINGING GROUP (*from boat that is crossing lake*)   "I Feel the Winds of God Today"

Sermonette   "There Are Two Seas," or an all-scriptural sermon, or Kahlil Gibran's "Sermon on the Mount."[38]

There Are Two Seas

There are two seas in Palestine.
One is fresh, and fish are in it. Splashes of green adorn its

banks. Trees spread their branches over it, and stretch out their thirsty roots to sip of its healing waters.

Along its shores the children play, as children played when He was there. He loved it. He could look across its silver surface when He spoke His parables. And on a rolling plain not far away He fed five thousand people.

The river Jordan makes this sea with sparkling water from the hills. Men build their houses near to it, and birds their nests; and every kind of life is happier because it is there.

The river Jordan flows on south into another sea.

Here is no splash of fish, no fluttering leaf, no song of birds, no children's laughter. Travelers choose another route, unless on urgent business. The air hangs heavy above its water, and neither man nor beast nor fowl will drink.

What makes this mighty difference in these neighbor seas?

Not the river Jordan. It empties the same good water into both. Not the soil in which they lie, not the country round about.

This is the difference. The Sea of Galilee receives but does not keep the Jordan. For every drop that flows into it another drop flows out.

The other sea is shrewder, hoarding its income jealously.

It will not be tempted into any generous impulse. Every drop it gets, it keeps.

The Sea of Galilee gives and lives. This other sea gives nothing. It is named The Dead.

There are two seas in Palestine.

There are two kinds of people in the world.

BRUCE BARTON[39]

Complete Silence   (*as boat leaves, allow five minutes*)
CONGREGATION (*leaves in silence*)

SOURCE NOTES

SOURCE NOTES

SECTION 1—WORSHIP

1. Throughout the years, and in other publications as well as in this one, I have been greatly indebted to the writings of Samuel F. Pugh, an outstanding minister-writer who served as editor of *World Call*, magazine of the Disciples of Christ (Christian Church). Once again, I wish to acknowledge his inspirational work.

2. From the *Book of Common Prayer*, p. 67.

3. By G. Edwin Osborne, *The Glory of Christian Worship*, p. 71.

4. By Jack Lundin. Reprinted from *Liturgies for Life*.

5. From *The Lamplighter* (Dr. Ray Montgomery, Editor), Speedway Christian Church, Indianapolis, Indiana.

6. By Dr. Chester Pennington in *The Christian Athlete*.

7. By Daniel Jenkins from *Equality and Excellence*, published by SCM Press, Ltd., London.

8. By James Peyton Hopkins, First Christian Church, Elsberry, Missouri.

9. By Georgia Harkness from *The Glory of God*.

SECTION 2—THE COMMUNION OF THE LORD'S SUPPER

10. By George Pease, *The Elder at the Lord's Table*, ed. Thomas Toler, p. 76.

SECTION 3—THE MINISTRY TO THE SICK

11. Samuel F. Pugh, *When You Are a Hospital Patient*, p. 10.

12. Edmund H. Babbitt, *Strength for Hospital Days*, p. 2.

13. Pugh, *When You Are a Hospital Patient*, p. 14.

14. Armin Frederick Bahnsen, *My Companion for Quiet Hours*, published by Church World Press, Inc., pp. 15, 16.

SECTION 4—THE WEDDING SERVICE

15. From *A Book of Worship for Free Churches*.

SECTION 5—THE FUNERAL SERVICE

16. W. Halsey Smith, quoted by the Rev. Robert J. Burdette in *The Wayside Altar*.

17. John Henry Newman.

18. Henry van Dyke.

19. Bishop Berggrav quoted in *The Christian Leader*, published by David C. Cook Publishing Company, December 30, 1956.

20. Leslie R. Smith, *From Sunset to Dawn*, p. 48.

21. Ibid., p. 41.

SECTION 6—HOLY WEEK SERVICES

22. Wallace Petty, *Minister's Service Handbook*, ed. James Dalton Morrison (New York: Harper and Brothers, 1937).

23. Author unknown. Reprinted from Christian Art Bulletin B12478, published by Warner Press.

24. *Divine Worship* (London: Epworth Press, 1935).

25. *A Book of Worship for Free Churches,* p. 372.

26. William E. Orchard, *Worship Resources,* ed. Charles L. Wallis (New York: Harper & Brothers), p. 99.

27. Richard K. Morton, *Worship Resources,* p. 99.

SECTION 7—CHRISTMAS SERVICES

28. Adapted from "Christmas Beatitudes," author unknown.

29. Developed over the years by James L. Christensen.

SECTION 8—SPECIAL CHURCH SERVICES

30. G. Edwin Osborne, *Christian Worship: A Service Book,* p. 138.

SECTION 9—PATRIOTIC SERVICES

31. John Hunter, *Divine Service for Public Worship.*

32. Morgan Phelps, *Prayers for Services,* p. 191.

33. From *The Book of Common Prayer of Ireland.*

34. Leslie Weatherhead, *Pulpit Digest,* July, 1952.

SECTION 10—OUTDOOR OCCASIONS

35. Chester Larue Hampton, *Worship Highways,* edited by Samuel W. Hutton, p. 184.

36. John C. Slimp, *Worship Highways.*

37. *World Call,* June, 1972.

38. Gibran's "Sermon on the Mount" is from *Jesus, The Son of Man,* published by Alfred A. Knopf, Inc., New York, p. 37.

39. From *McCall's* magazine, April, 1928. Used by permission.

INDEX

INDEX